[日英対訳]

日本人のこころ

Heart & Soul
of the Japanese

増補・改訂版

山久瀬洋二＝著
マイケル・クーニー＝訳

英語で語る

日本人の価値、そして思い

IBC パブリッシング

装　　幀　見増勇介、関屋晶子〈ym design〉

翻訳協力　Jamaes M. Vardaman〈14 流 Drifting Away 〉

本書は 2011 年に小社から刊行された、対訳ニッポン双書『日本人のこころ』を増補・改訂したものです。

はじめに

　本書は、日本人が伝統的に抱き続けてきた価値観や思いをどのように英語で伝えるかということを、価値観を14のテーマに分類して、まとめたものです。

　文化は、国や地域によってさまざまです。ですから、日本人が素晴らしいと思っている価値観でも、海外ではそれが不可解であったり、時には全く違う観点からマイナスに評価されてしまうことがあるかもしれません。例えば、日本人が謙遜して遠慮すると、アメリカ人はその人を控えめで社会性のある人と思うのではなく、自信がなくフレンドリーではない人だと評価してしまうこともあるのです。だからこそ、自分の文化について英語で語る力が必要になります。

　つまり、価値観は決して善悪の基準ではなく、あくまでも相対的なものなのです。しかし、それが相手側の善悪の基準により、時と場合によって誤解され判断されるリスクがあるわけです。ですから、我々も自らの価値観をただ相手に押し付けることは危険だと思わなければなりません。

　自らの文化の土台となる価値観は、その国のアイデンティティでもあり、時にはプライドの源泉でもあるはずです。ということは同じように日本とは異なる価値観がその国や地域に住む人が大切に培っている常識となっていることも多々あるわけです。ですから、本書で語る日本の価値観や日本人の心の原点は、決してお国自慢ではないのだということを意識してほしいのです。

　一方で、そんな日本人ならではの価値観に従って、どう世界で活躍し、貢献できるかということを考えれば、それはそれで素晴らしいことといえましょう。なぜならば異なる価値観が混ざることで、よりお互いの理解が増え、そこから一つの文化背景だけでは創造できないシナジーが醸し出されるからです。

この本で紹介する日本人の心を形成する価値観の中には、ともすれば日本人にとっても忘れ去られがちなものもあるかもしれません。しかし、これらの価値観が日本人の行動やコミュニケーションスタイルの土台となり、気付かれないままにも受け継がれてきていることは確かです。ということは、本書を通して自らのルーツを見つめ直すこともできるかもしれません。その上で、もし何か海外の人との間でコミュニケーションが難しいと思ったとき、そうしたルーツがいかに自分の行動に影響を与えているかを探れば、相手との溝を埋める手段にもなるはずです。

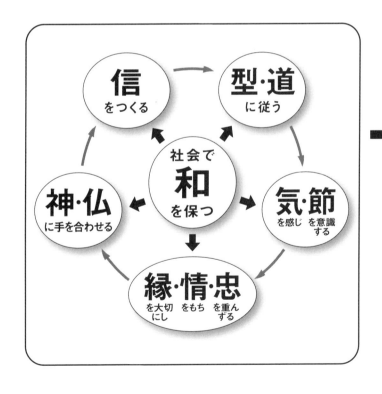

そしてまた、価値観は時と共に変化もします。今回はそのことを踏まえ、現在を生きる我々の価値観についても触れてみました。その上で現在の価値観にも微妙に何世紀にもわたって受け継がれた伝統的な思いの残り香があることにぜひ気づいてほしいのです。

　日本はともすれば世界の中でも最も「ミステリアス」な国だと言われてきました。その原因は欧米の人からみると真逆な行動が日本人にとっては当然の常識となっているからに他なりません。そんな一面を、本書を通して理解するのも面白いはずです。
　人は自分のことを論理的に語ることができにくいものです。あまりにも当たり前のことは、説明しにくいものです。英語であればなおさらです。本書がそんな困難を克服する一助となれば幸いです。

山久瀬洋二

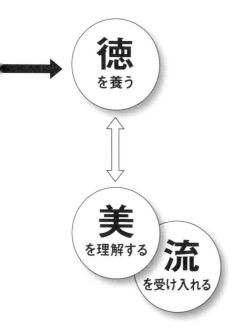

目次 Contents

9

1

和

Harmony

和

「和」とは、そのまま訳せばharmonyです。

「和」はまた日本を表す別の表現でもあります。たとえば日本食のことを、日本人は和食ともいいます。日本の伝統的な服は和服と呼びます。

「和」とは、人と人とがいかに心地よく、共に過ごし、働くかということを表す価値観です。

日本は伝統的に、限られた土地を皆で耕作して、生活をしてきた**農耕社会**によって成り立ってきました。この社会を成り立たせるためには、村人が自らのニーズよりも、村全体のニーズを考え、他の人々と行動を共にして稲を植え、収穫をしなければなりません。

したがって、日本には、個人の力量や行動を価値基準の中心におく狩猟社会や移民社会とは異なる、常に相手との絆を気遣い、**グループで行動する**ことをよしとする価値基準が育まれました。それが「和」という価値観なのです。

日本人にとって「和」は、日本人の心の中に培われた全ての価値観の要となる考え方なのです。

聖徳太子が著したとされる日本最初の17条憲法にも、「和をもって尊しとなす」とあるのは興味深いことです。

配慮

「配慮」とは、「**心を配る**」という考え方です。実際、同じ意味で「心配り」あるいは「気配り」という言葉があります。

Harmony

While the Chinese character for *wa* means "harmony," it is also used to mean "Japan." For example, Japanese cuisine is known as *wa-shoku* and Japanese clothing is known as *wa-fuku*.

"Harmony" is a basic value defined as the ability of people to cooperate and work together well.

Japan is a country whose traditions developed out of an **agricultural society** where people were forced to work closely together on a limited amount of land. In order to maintain this type of society, the needs of the village were more important than the needs of the individual, as all labored together to plant the rice and harvest the crop.

Therefore, as opposed to hunter- or immigrant-based societies, where a high value is placed on the power or actions of the individual, a society developed in Japan where the value is placed on understanding those with whom one must interact and on **taking action in groups**. That is the definition of *wa*.

Wa is at the heart of what has been necessary to nurture everything in the Japanese value system.

Consideration

Hairyo means to **share one's heart**. In fact, *kokoro-kubari* or *ki-kubari* (both literally meaning "heart sharing") have the same meaning as *hairyo*.

　「和」を保つには、相手がどのように感じ、行動したいかを考えて、その意思に対して自らも対応できるようにしなければなりません。たとえ、相手のしたいことが、自分とは異なっていても、**対立しないような**対応のしかたを考えなければならないのです。そうした考え方を「配慮」と呼びます。

　たとえば、直接反対の意思を表示するのではなく、その人の前では曖昧に答えておいて、その後相手が信頼する人物を通して、間接的に自らの意図を伝え、相手との**摩擦**を少なくすることも「配慮」の一つです。

　ただ、この日本人の行動は、日本では「和」を保つ妙薬かもしれませんが、日本人でない人からみると、なぜ自分に直接話してくれないのかという疑念を相手に与え、**不信感**をあおる原因になることもあるのです。

　「和」の心の表し方としての「配慮」という価値観は、日本人にとってはとても大切です。その価値観を外国の人の思考方法に合わせた行動で示すためには、**相手の文化の中で**、そうした時にどのような行動をとるかということを、事前に知っておく必要があるのです。

謙譲と謙遜

　「和」をもって人とつき合うとき、お互いが自我を出しあって、自らの能力を強調し合ってばかりいると、物事がうまく進みません。日本人はこういうとき、むしろ**自らの能力を抑え**、相手に敬意を払いながら、相手との関係を構築します。この自分を**へりくだり**、相手に対してあえて自らの能力を表明しない考え方を「謙譲」といいます。

To maintain *wa*, one must take action based on how the person one is dealing with feels and what that person wishes to do. For example, if what the other person wishes to do is different from what you wish to do, you must find a way to take action indirectly **to avoid confrontation**. This way of thinking is called *hairyo*.

Following up on this thought, instead of expressing an opposing opinion directly to a person, one might use an intermediary whom the person trusts to convey one's intent and thereby reduce **friction**. This is another example of *hairyo*.

While this is a very effective means of maintaining *wa* by Japanese in Japan, non-Japanese might very well take a different view of these actions, wondering why someone chose not to talk to him directly, and thereby fostering the potential for **mistrust**.

As an expression of *wa*, *hairyo* is an important basic value for the Japanese. For this basic value to be effectively used with non-Japanese, however, it is necessary to understand beforehand how to act based on the particular circumstances of the time and place **within the context of the culture of the other person**.

Modesty

When using *wa* as the basis for a relationship, things will not go smoothly if both parties egotistically emphasize their own capabilities. A Japanese person would in fact **downplay his own capabilities** while paying respect to the other person and build the relationship in that way. This concept of **putting oneself below** another and not presuming to show one's capabilities is

相手も、「私は何もわかりませんが」といわれると、それを言葉通りには受け止めません。逆に日本では、能力のある人ほど、自分のことを低く表現することがよいこととされているために、このようにいう相手は、かえって尊敬されるのです。

この「謙譲」の価値観を実際の言葉遣いで表すとき、人は「謙遜する」という表現を使います。この言葉こそは、日本人の極めて大切な行動原理となっているのです。

「謙遜する」という行為は、時には家族や会社の同僚を紹介するときに使われます。自分の子どもを紹介するとき、**「何もできない愚息ですが」**などといって紹介する習わしがそれにあたります。

自らの能力を率直に表現することをよしとする文化背景からきた外国人には、この日本人の行動原理がわからず、戸惑いを覚えることがよくあるようです。

「実るほど頭を垂れる稲穂かな」という日本人の好きな言葉があります。また、**「能ある鷹は爪を隠す」**という言葉も有名です。これは全て「謙遜」することの美学を伝える言葉なのです。

謙虚

「謙虚」とは、「謙譲」や「謙遜」の精神をもっている心の状態を示す言葉です。すなわち、知っていることを表に出さず、常に自分はまだ何も知らず、学ぶことがたくさんあるのだという姿勢で物事に向かう心を示しているので

called *kenjō*.

One cannot take the words at their face value when one is told: "I don't know anything." In Japan, the greater the capabilities of a person, the more modestly he will state those capabilities, and thus in fact such persons are more respected.

When stating the value of *kenjō* in a sentence, it is common to use the word *kenson*, as in *kenson suru* ("**being modest**"). *Kenson* is a very important word in Japanese, reflecting the basic principles of the culture.

The concept of *kenson* is often used when introducing a member of one's family or company. This is evident in the phrase "**good-for-nothing son**" when introducing one's son, for example.

It seems that much confusion is created by the Japanese using this principle of *kenson* with non-Japanese whose cultures value **straight-forward expression** of one's capabilities.

"**The heavier the stock of rice, the more its head is lowered**" is an expression well liked by the Japanese. "**A wise hawk hides its talons**" is another well-known phrase. These all convey the beauty of the concept of *kenson*.

Modest

Kenkyo means having the heart of *kenjō* or *kenson*. In other words, instead of showing off what one knows, one always conveys the impression that one knows nothing and still has much to learn. This does not mean that one is trying to take advantage

す。これは、決して相手に自分の能力を隠して油断させるというような考え方ではないのです。

逆に、学ぶ者がとらなければならない真摯な態度であり、「謙虚」であることを日本人は美徳としているのです。あの人は「謙虚」な人だといえば、それは褒め言葉なのです。

「謙虚」の「謙」は**へりくだる**という意味をもつ漢字で、相手に対して自らの位置を低くおき、相手に**敬意を払う**ことを意味する文字です。「虚」は中に何もない状態を意味します。すなわち、「謙虚」とは、心を「無」にして、相手に敬意をもって接する心がけを示しているのです。

これこそ、**和をもって人と接する**ための最も大切な心がけなのです。

ですから、欧米の人には、日本人がへりくだった態度で接しているとき、それを誤解せずに、自分への敬意と捉えてもらえればいいのですが。

遠慮

「和」を保つために最も考えなければならないことは、相手のことを 慮 (おもんぱか) る気持ちです。相手の状況を考えて、自らの行動を抑制し、相手に**迷惑にならない**ようにすることを「遠慮」といいます。

遠慮の「遠」は遠くを、そして「慮」は思いめぐらすこと

of others by hiding what one knows.

Rather, Japanese believe that one must have the **virtue** of being *kenkyo* if one is serious about learning. Calling a person *kenkyo* is an expression of praise.

The first Chinese character of *ken* in *kenkyo* means to **lower oneself**; in other words, to put oneself in a lower position and **pay respect** to the other person. The second Chinese character, *kyo*, means to be in a state of "nothingness." Put another way, *kenkyo* means to put one's heart in a state of *mu*, or nothingness, while maintaining an attitude of respect towards the other person.

This is one of the most important aspects of interacting with other persons **in the spirit of *wa***.

Therefore, when Japanese put themselves in a more modest position when dealing with Westerners, they hope that this is taken as a sign of respect and their intentions are not misunderstood.

Reserve

To maintain *wa*, it is always very important to give **careful consideration** to the feelings of the person with whom one is dealing. Understanding the circumstances of the other person and controlling one's actions so as **not to cause trouble** to that person is called *enryo*.

The first Chinese character of *en* in *enryo* means "distant,"

を意味します。つまり、つねに先に思いを巡らして、相手に対応する心がけが「遠慮」なのです。躊躇hesitationという言葉がありますが、これは何かをすれば**状況が悪くなる**のではと恐れて行動を抑制することを意味します。

　それに対して「遠慮」は、むしろそうなる前に**しっかりと相手のことを考えて**、相手のために行動を差し控える未来に向けた心構えなのです。

　相手に聞くまでもなく、自らが相手の気持ちを判断して、たとえば「今この話をすると相手が不快だろうから、遠慮して別の機会にしておこう」などと考えるのです。

　言葉をもって明快に自らのニーズを伝え、それに対応することをよしとする欧米の文化からしてみると、この「遠慮」という考え方を理解することは困難です。躊躇がさらに未来の行動へと延長すると思えばわかりやすいのかもしれませんが、国際舞台では、日本人はついつい「遠慮」をしすぎて、自らの意思を伝えるチャンスを失っているようでもありますね。

　現在では、「遠慮」という言葉をそのまま、「禁止する」と同じ意味に使うことも多々あります。「タバコはご遠慮ください」といえば、禁煙を丁寧に相手に伝えることになるのです。

場

　「遠慮」という考え方を理解するために必要なのがこの「場」という概念です。「場」とはいうまでもなく場所を意

while the second character of *ryo* means "to think about." In other words, always thinking ahead about how to deal with other people is *enryo*. The word *chūcho* means "to hesitate," and is used in describing a situation in which a person refrains from taking action due to fear that **circumstances will worsen**.

Enryo, on the other hand, means thinking ahead before a situation develops, **taking fully into account the other person**, and then **refraining from** action based on those circumstances.

Without asking, one should be able to judge the feelings of the other person and decide if *enryo* is necessary. For example, "If I bring this up now, I'll make the other person feel uncomfortable, so I'll wait until another time."

In a culture where people are expected to speak up and make their needs known, with action being taken based on those requests, it is difficult for Westerners to understand the concept of *enryo*. Westerners, they may be able to understand *enryo* as an extension of *chūcho*, or hesitation, but too often the Japanese lose the chance to speak out on issues on the international stage due to their tendency towards *enryo*.

Nowadays the word *enryo* is also often used to mean "prohibited." For example, *tabako wa go-enryo kudasai* is a polite way of telling people that smoking is prohibited.

Place, Situation

To understand the thinking behind *enryo*, the concept of *ba* is necessary. It goes without saying that *ba* refers to "place." What

味します。そして、どういう場所でどのような行動をする
かということを**暗に示した**のが「場」という概念なのです。

　この「場」という考え方は、欧米でもあるようです。た
とえば、結婚式を例にとれば、正式に教会や神社で行う儀
式と、その後で披露宴などのパーティーでの人々の行動は
自ずと違ってきます。儀式の間は**しきたり**に従い、パーテ
ィーでは比較的自由に人々は交流します。すなわち、「場」
が違えば、それぞれ「場」に合った行動が求められるので
す。

　日本では日本人の価値観や行動様式に従って、外国人に
は見えない「場」がたくさんあります。お客さんとの正式
な打合せの「場」での態度や、上司の前という「場」でのも
のの言い方、または**くだけた**お酒の席という「場」での発
言など、「場」によって人の行動が細かく変わり、時には
その「場」の状況によって、人は行動を差し控え「遠慮」す
ることもあるのです。

　「場をわきまえる」という言葉がありますが、「場」の状
況をしっかりと理解して、その時に何をすべきかを的確に
判断することが、**日本での礼儀作法**の第一歩といえます。

　微妙な「場」の違いに気付かない外国人は、時には**不作
法**をしてしまうかもしれません。

間

　「間」は時間的、物理的な距離を意味する言葉です。特
に二つのものの間を示す言葉としても使われます。

actions happen in what place is **implicit** within the concept of *ba*.

The idea of *ba*, "place," also exists in the West. For example, in the case of a wedding, the actions of people at the ceremony at the church or temple are different from people's actions at the reception afterwards. At the ceremony there are **strict practices** to follow, while at the reception people interact in a relatively free manner. In other words, because the *ba*, "place," is different, different actions are required.

There are many *ba* in Japan where the basic values and actions of the Japanese are employed, and these *ba* may be difficult for the non-Japanese to understand. The words and actions of a formal meeting with a customer will differ from those in a meeting with one's boss, and will differ again in the **informal** atmosphere of a night out on the town. At times, the concept of *enryo* will be necessary within the context of a particular *ba*.

The expression *ba wo wakimaeru* means to clearly understand the circumstances of a particular *ba*. Being able to make proper judgments about what to do based on the particular time and place is a first step towards truly grasping the basics of **Japanese etiquette**.

Sometimes a non-Japanese, not understanding the subtleties of a particular *ba*, will commit a **faux pas**.

Space, Interval

Ma means a space or interval in terms of time or distance. It is especially used as an indicator of space between two things.

和

日本人は、伝統的に人と人との間での時間的、物理的な距離を強く意識する習慣がありました。それが「間」という概念となったのです。

たとえば、**封建時代**には、身分の高い人に近づくことはタブーでした。高貴な人と話をするときは、かなり距離をおき、低い位置から話をすることが**礼儀**でした。直接話をすることができず、その人に近い人物にメッセージを託して思いを伝えることも頻繁にありました。

「間」という概念をみると、そうした日本人の伝統的な考え方が現在にも影響を与えていることがよくわかります。

相手に対して何か深刻な事柄や、大切な依頼などを伝えるとき、即座に直接その人に伝えるのではなく、**適当な時**を考えて、場合によっては間接的に**人を介して**話してもらうことは、日本の社会では今も普通に行われているのです。

また、相手との**緊張関係を解く**ときも、その場で相手に話しかけずに、多少時間をおいてからゆっくりとその人に接してゆこうとします。このとき「**少し間をおいて**」と日本人はいうのです。

実際、会話の場でも、日本人は会話と会話の間の沈黙が比較的長く、外国人がそれに耐えられず困ってしまうことも多いようです。

日本人は、伝統的に長い沈黙に慣れていて、そこにも「間」という概念が働いているのかもしれません。

会話の間の沈黙は国や文化、言語によって異なる。日本人は欧米人に比べると、沈黙への耐久力が長いとされる。

中庸

極端を嫌い、常にいろいろな考え方の**中間に自らをおいて**行動する知恵を、「中庸」といいます。

Traditionally, the Japanese had a strong sense of the distance between people in terms of time and physical space. That became the basis for the concept of *ma*.

For example, during **feudal times** it was taboo to approach people of high rank. **Etiquette** required that one speak to such persons from a considerable distance and from a physically lower position. In fact, it was common to not approach such persons directly and instead use an intermediary to pass on messages.

It is easy to see many examples today of how the concept of *ma* continues to influence Japanese society.

When one has a serious matter to report or an important request to make, it is usual to not act immediately but rather wait for a more **appropriate time** or **use an intermediary** to pass on the message.

Again, when seeking to **ease tensions** with a person, it is common to forego a contentious subject and leave some time before bringing it up. In this case, the Japanese say *sukoshi ma wo oite* ("**take a little break**").

Even within a single conversation, the Japanese like to take breaks, allowing for periods of silence, and it seems that these silences can be uncomfortable for the non-Japanese.

The Japanese are used to long periods of silence, and that is probably because the concept of *ma* is at work.

Moderation

The ability to stay away from the extreme and to always **seek out the middle road** describes the concept of *chūyō*.

　バランスよくどちらの考え方にも耳を貸し、よいところをとりながら物事を進める方法は、「和」をもって人と付き合い、組織などを運営してゆくための知恵だと日本人の多くは思っています。

　もちろん、この考え方には弱点もあります。強いリーダーシップを発揮しにくく、そうした個性そのものを否定する側面が、「中庸」という考え方にはあるからです。

　日本で会社や組織のリーダーを「あの人は**調整型の人だ**」と評価することがあります。それは、人と人との関係を大切にし、地道に異なる意見を調整しながら組織をまとめてゆく人格を意味する表現です。そうした人格の人が重んじる価値観が、この「中庸」という価値観なのです。

　物事を急いで決めず、じっくりとより多くの人の意見を参考にしながら進めてゆくこの方法は、今のグローバルな時代に適しているかどうかはわかりません。しかし、「中庸」のよいところは、リスクを最大限回避できることでしょう。

　実は、西欧の倫理学の原点ともいえるアリストテレスも極端を悪として、「中庸」を尊ぶことを説いています。

　現代社会では、「中庸」の考えを取り入れながらも、迅速に行動できる方法が必要なのかもしれません。それは、**いうまでもなく**、日々、人々とできるだけまめにコミュニケーションをとっておくことでしょう。

　どんな価値にも強い側面と弱い側面があり、「中庸」もその価値の使い方によって、効果もあり、逆になることもあるはずです。そのことを知って、うまく「中庸」の発想を実践することが、必要なのかもしれません。

For the Japanese, *wa* ("harmony") is maintained in an organization by working with others in a balanced way in which all points of view are carefully considered before taking the best of those ideas and moving forward.

Of course this approach also has its own weaknesses. It becomes more difficult to exhibit strong leadership, as such individuality itself is to be avoided when employing *chūyō*.

In Japan, one means of appraising leadership is to describe someone as **having a "modulating style."** This expression describes a personality capable of managing an organization by taking all relationships seriously and modulating opinions outside of the mainstream to fit with the whole. The respect paid to such leaders reflects the value placed on *chūyō*.

In a global age where speed is the priority, it is not clear whether this approach of not quickly making decisions and of taking the time to carefully consider the opinions of many people, fits. However, the biggest advantage of *chūyō* may lie in its avoidance of risk.

It was Aristotle, the source of much of Western philosophy, who said that the extreme is bad and that the moderate should be respected.

In today's world, it may be necessary to come up with the means of employing *chūyō* while also taking action with some degree of speed. **It goes without saying that** in order to accomplish this, the most important factor is day-to-day communication with people.

In any value, there are strong points and weak points. In the case of *chūyō*, it is also true that depending on how it is used, it will be effective sometimes and not so effective at other times. Knowing when it is appropriate to use *chūyō* is essential.

低頭

　「低頭」とは、頭を低く下げてお礼を言ったりお詫びを
したりすることを意味する言葉です。多くは、「平身低頭」
という熟語として使われ、その場合は、何も言い訳せず、
しっかりと頭を下げてお詫びすることを意味します。

　日本人は、欧米の人と比較すると、すぐに人に謝りま
す。たとえ、自分に非がなくても「謙遜」し、さらにその
ような状況を生み出した原因は自分の対応にも問題があ
ったはずだという姿勢で、トラブルを回避するためにまず
相手にお詫びするのです。

　これは、日本人が人と共存してゆくための知恵でもあっ
たのです。すなわち、謝ることで、まず相手との緊張を解
き、その後で和やかな雰囲気の中で今後のことを相談した
り、何が起きたかを語り合うために、まずは謝り合うので
す。

英語のsorryは謝る
だけでなく、トラブ
ルにおちいった相
手に同情するときも
つかう。Apologize
はまさに「お詫び」
のための言葉。

　たとえ自分は悪くないと思った場合でも、日本ではその
正当性を一方的に強調することはタブーです。何かを指
摘されたとき、お詫びがなく、その原因や理由だけを説明
すると、「いい訳ばかりして」と捉えられてしまうことも
多くあります。

　まず「謙虚」に頭を下げて、その後で「間」をおいて、
「場」を変えて、時には人を介して本当のことを伝えてゆ
くことが、日本人がよく行うコミュニケーションスタイル
なのです。

　何よりもお詫びをすることで、相手の気持ちが収まり、
そこから人間関係を構築できるという風に日本人は考え
るわけです。

To Lower One's Head

Teitō means to deeply lower one's head as a sign of gratitude or apology. It is often used in the expression *heishin teitō* ("to **prostrate oneself**"), which is employed when one makes a full apology with absolutely no excuses.

Compared to Westerners, the Japanese tend to be quicker to make apologies. For example, even if he has done no wrong, a Japanese may exhibit a *kenson* ("modest") attitude and offer an apology in order to avoid trouble, indicating that he may have been **remiss** in his follow-up to determine the cause of the issue in question.

This is a capability that the Japanese have developed in order to get along well with each other. In other words, first one will try to calm down the other person through an apology and then from that point, in this more relaxed atmosphere, discuss what has happened.

Even if you are not in the wrong, it is taboo in Japan to **make a one-sided argument** about the fact that you are in the right. It is common for someone who simply argues the logic of his position, without making an apology, to be judged as "just an excuse maker."

The communication style often employed by the Japanese calls for a person to first **modestly lower his head**, then wait a certain period of time before perhaps changing location and using an intermediary to get across his truly intended message.

Above all else, the Japanese feel that an apology will help to **settle down** the emotions of the other person, allowing the relationship to be developed from there.

　そうした意味では、日本人にとって、「お詫び」は、人間同士がよい関係を構築するための最初の儀式でもあるのです。

根回し

　人との「和」を保ち、賢く自らの意見を**公で発表**するために、日本人は適切な「場」を選び、「間」も考慮して慎重に人とその情報を**共有**してゆきます。こうした日本人の行動様式の典型が「**根回し**」という意思伝達方法なのです。

アメリカのロビー活動（lobbying）は、まさに政治家の票集め、意見の具申のための「根回し」といえる。

　会議の「場」でいきなりプレゼンテーションを行うと、場合によっては上司や関係者と意見の対立を生むリスクがあります。それを避けるために、関係する人に事前にその情報を伝えたり、必要に応じて提案内容を調整することを「**根回し**」というのです。

　「根回し」が首尾よく行われていれば、会議の「場」で紛糾することなく、案件が承認されるわけです。

　「根回し」は**非公式**であるのみならず、時には夕食やゴルフなどの会合といった職場から離れたプライベートな「場」で行われることもあります。

　そして、「根回し」をしっかりと**繰り返す**ことで、人と公然と対立せずに、情報が共有され、企画やアイデアに関する情報が共有されるのです。

　そもそも、根回しとは、木を移植するときに、根を掘り起こし、それを傷つけないように丸く包んで移動させる方

For the Japanese, an apology is the first "ceremony" to take place between two parties, making a starting point in developing a relationship.

Lobbying

In order to preserve harmony (*wa*) when going "**on the record**" with an opinion, the Japanese will cautiously **share** information with others after careful consideration of the place and the timing. A very typical Japanese form of communicating one's will in this situation would be *nemawashi* (literally "**loosening the roots**").

If one presents a proposal for the first time right at a meeting, there is a risk that one's superiors or others affected by the proposal will have a different opinion. Avoiding this risk by consulting prior to the meeting with key persons and adjusting one's proposal as necessary is called *nemawashi* ("**lobbying**").

If one has done a thorough job of *nemawashi*, there should be little opposition at the meeting and the proposal should be approved.

It is common for *nemawashi* to take place **outside the office**, perhaps over dinner or while playing golf or at some other private setting (*ba*).

Through the repetition of *nemawashi*, there will naturally be fewer conflicts, with better sharing of plans and ideas.

The original meaning of *nemawashi* is to "loosen the roots," or in other words, to carefully dig a circle around the roots in

法のことです。

　すなわち、木を移植するときと同じように、関係者一人一人と話すことによって、人の輪をつくり、それを包み込んで公式の場に持ち込む方法が「根回し」なのです。

　「根回し」は今でも日本の組織のあちこちで実践されています。外国の人が「根回し」の外におかれないためには、日本人とより気軽に接触し、時には夜一緒にお酒を飲むなどして、日本人の輪の中に入ってゆくことが肝要です。

　これは、日本では公式な場だけではなく、個々人のレベルでの密なコミュニケーションがいかに大切かを物語る、**象徴的な概念**であるともいえそうです。

order to preserve them when moving a plant or tree.

Similarly, when conducting *nemawashi* for a proposal, one is trying to carefully create a circle of consensus among the key people involved to move the proposal unscathed to the formal setting of a meeting.

Even now the use of *nemawashi* is quite common in organizations in Japan. It is important for non-Japanese to also move into "the circle of consensus" when conducting business in Japan by spending more time in *nemawashi* over drinks or in other informal settings.

This says just how important informal, one-on-one settings are in communicating in Japan. *Nemawashi* is indeed a **representative concept** of Japanese values.

2

Form,
Way of Doing Things

型

　「和」という価値観で、農耕社会を基軸とする日本社会でのコミュニケーションの方法について説明しました。そして、自分の考えや能力を強く主張することなく社会を運営してゆくために、日本人が発展させてきた価値観が、ここに紹介する「型」という考え方です。

　古代から、農業での豊作を神に感謝し、人と人との**絆を強くするために**、人々はさまざまな儀式をつくってゆきました。その後、身分や階級制度が社会に浸透する中で、さらに人と人との上下関係を具体的に表すための作法やマナーが生み出されます。

　儀式や作法は、全ての人がその様式に従うために、それぞれの「場」での行動様式、すなわち「型」が生み出され、次第に社会の多くの場面で、さまざまな「型」が尊重されるようになったのです。

　今では、「型」は日本人の生活様式、行動のいたるところにみることができます。ビジネスでの名刺交換、相撲での**取組前の儀式**、そしてごく日常でいうならば、お酒の席での杯の受け方やつぎ方など。

　また、武道や伝統の専門領域のことを習得するためには、まずそこで培われた「型」を学ぶことが要求されます。「型」をマスターしてこそ、人々は次のステップに進むことができるのです。「型」を習得するという価値観は、日本人が物事を進めるにあたって、どのように対処すべきかという方程式をまず理解しようという意識を植え付けます。まず、行動し、**試行錯誤**をしながら進めるのではなく、「いかにhow」の答えを見つけてから進もうとする考え方を日本人は好むのです。

Form

We have already discussed how *wa* ("harmony") was an essential social value in the communication style of feudal Japan. Here we will introduce *kata* ("form"), another Japanese value that promotes social cooperation over one's individual thoughts or capabilities.

In ancient times, people in agricultural communities gave thanks to the gods, creating various ceremonies that helped to **strengthen bonds** with other people. Later, as a class system developed, additional forms of etiquette came into being as a means of expressing the difference in rank among people.

To ensure that all people would appropriately follow the various ceremonies and etiquette, the concept of *kata* developed, whereby a particular *kata* ("form") would be followed at a particular place and time.

Nowadays, one can see *kata* in action in all aspects of Japanese life. The exchange of name cards, the **pre-bout rituals** of sumo, even the relatively mundane act of pouring and receiving a cup of sake—these are all examples.

In *budō* ("martial arts") or in other traditional disciplines, one must first **cultivate *kata***. The more quickly one is able to master *kata*, the quicker one will advance to the next step. For the Japanese, before tackling a project, it is essential that they first understand the process by which that project will be completed. It is not proper to take random actions, trying to accomplish things through **trial and error**; rather one must first understand the answer to the question: How?

　「型」は、日本人の行動様式、ビジネスの進め方を知る上でも大切な価値観なのです。

作法

　「作法」とは、昔から定まった伝統的な行動様式を指す言葉です。封建時代は、身分制度がありました。身分の高い人に対してどのように振る舞うかは、最も知っておかなければならない行動様式です。

　「作法」は、まさに「型」にのっとっています。ちょうど、欧米の人が握手をする習慣があるように、日本では人と対面し、交流するときに日本ならでは習慣に従って行動します。そして、日本には封建時代以来受け継いできたさまざまな習慣が、現代社会の人間関係にも投影されているのです。

　たとえば、茶道において、どこに客人を案内し、どのようにしてお湯を沸かし、お茶を点て振る舞うか、全て**定められた方式があり**ます。

　また、ビジネスの世界では、ものを売る側が買う側に対して、敬語を使い、より深くお辞儀をするなど、さまざまな敬意を表すための作法があります。また、会社では上司と部下との間で、部下が上司に対してどのように行動するかという作法があります。

　多くの日本人は、自分が目に見えない作法に従って、行動様式を変化させていることすら、それがあまりにも**当たり前すぎて**、気づかないかもしれません。しかし、海外から来た人が日本人をよく観察すると、不思議に思える行動を発見します。なぜ、ここで何度もお辞儀をしているのか。どうしてこの人は**背筋を伸ばして**固まったようにし

Kata is an important concept in understanding how the Japanese operate in business and in other fields.

Etiquette

Sahō describes forms of behavior that have been set by society for a long period of time. There was a class system in place in Japan during the feudal period. Knowing how to behave towards a person of higher rank was of the utmost importance.

Sahō means doing what fits into the right *kata* ("form"). Just as Westerners greet each other with a handshake, so do the Japanese have their accepted forms of behavior when they meet each other. The etiquette of the Japanese today reflects practices that have been in place since feudal times.

For example, in the case of the tea ceremony, every act is carefully **choreographed**, from where people sit, to how the water is boiled, to how the tea is prepared, and so on.

Again, in the business world, one can observe *sahō* in action as the seller employs polite language and bows often as he shows various forms of respect to the buyer. Another case would be the social setting of a company, where a subordinate will use particular *sahō* with his boss.

For most Japanese, *sahō* is an **ingrained** pattern of behavior that affects their day-to-day actions without them even being aware of it. However, for people who come from overseas, some of these practices may appear puzzling. Why is someone bowing so many times in a particular setting? Or at another time, why is someone sitting **ramrod straight**? But for the Japanese, they are

て座っているのかなど。場所や状況に応じて、日本人はそうした作法に従っているのです。

行儀

「行儀」をそのまま翻訳すると、マナーという英語につながります。

その意味の通り、「行儀」とは公の「場」で人と接するときのエチケットやマナーのことで、どこの国でも親がまず子どもに教えなければならない常識です。

そして、マナーよく振る舞うためには、どこの国でも日本の「型」に似た行動様式があるはずです。

日本での行儀を「型」という価値観からみた場合、常に学ぶ者の教える者に対する敬意の払い方が、**細かく組み込**まれていることが分かります。

姿勢を正して、きちっと座り、教えてもらう間は言葉を挟まず黙って学び、質問があれば後で尋ね、教える者にチャレンジするような態度はとらず、常に謙虚な姿勢で接することが要求されます。

日本に中国から伝わった言葉で、「**青は藍より出でて藍より青し**」という言葉があります。元々藍からつくられた青色は、藍よりも深くて美しい青になっているという意味で、しっかりと修行をして、師よりも深い技量を身につけることの美徳を語った言葉です。

たとえ習う者が、師を超えたとしても、日本人は一生師に感謝し、師に対して**最高の敬意**を払いつづけるのが、正しい行儀なのです。

simply following the *sahō* that is appropriate for that place and circumstance.

Manners

The direct translation of *gyōgi* into English is "manners."

In keeping with this translation, *gyōgi* is the etiquette, or manners, followed in public places as a matter of generally accepted practice and taught by all parents to their children.

As in Japan, all countries have their own *kata* ("forms"), which are in place to ensure that correct manners are followed.

One can easily understand the **painstaking way** in which a student pays respect to a teacher in Japan if one views *gyōgi* through the concept of *kata* ("form").

The student sits properly, doesn't talk during the lesson, asks questions only later, and does not take a challenging attitude towards the teacher.

In Japan, there is a saying taken from the Chinese: "**The blue of an indigo is bluer than indigo.**" What this means is that although the blue dye made from the indigo plant, it is in fact a deeper and more beautiful blue than indigo. In the same way, if a student studies seriously, he may become more skillful than his teacher.

Once a student manages to pass his teacher, the Japanese believe that it is correct *gyōgi* to give thanks to the teacher and continue to treat him **with the utmost respect**.

修練

　「型」を学ぶときは、**何度も同じことを繰り返しながら**、柔道での体の動きや**習字での筆の使い方**、あるいは踊るときの振る舞い方などを習得します。もちろん、「型」にはそれぞれ合理的な理由があったはずです。しかし、それがいかに合理的であるかを理解するためには、ただ黙々と「型」によって表現されるパターンを覚えてゆく必要があります。

　教える者は、得てして理由を伝えることなく、教える者が**納得するまで**、学習者に「型」を教え込みます。日本には伝統的にフィードバックという文化がなく、学ぶ者は教える者を信じ、その指示に問いかけることなく従ってゆきました。

　「型」の習得には時には何年もの**修業**期間が必要です。そしてしっかりと「型」を学んだ後に、はじめて学習者はその合理性に気付き、そこからさらに技量を発展させてゆくのです。

　この「型」を学ぶ厳しい過程を「修練」といいます。そして、「修練」というものの考え方は、ビジネスのノウハウを習得してゆく上での、上司と部下の関係にもみてとることができるのです。フィードバックがなく、ただ厳しく指導する上司は、最近でこそ少なくなりました。とはいえ、今なお、欧米人が日本人を上司にもったとき、フィードバックの少なさに**戸惑う**ことがよくあります。

　確かに、このフィードバックの少ない日本流の指導方法は、欧米のマネージメントとは根本的に異なっているようです。

英語の"Just do it."は型や背景を学ぶより、まず行動を、という修練とは対局にある言葉。

Discipline

When learning a new *kata* ("form"), one will repeat the same action **numerous times**, whether it is a judo throw or the **strokes of a calligraphy brush** or the steps of a dance. Of course there is ultimately a logic to all *kata*, but in order to truly understand that logic, it is necessary for the student to continue to silently repeat the action.

The teacher does not tell the student why something must be done in a certain way; he simply continues to have the student repeat the action until he, the teacher, is **satisfied**. In Japan traditionally there is no culture of "feedback." The student trusts the teacher and follows the directions of the teacher without questioning.

In certain cases, it may be necessary to spend many years **in training** to master *kata*. Only then, after the *kata* has been mastered, does the student really first understand the true logic of his movements, and then from there he may further develop his skill.

This demanding process of learning a *kata* is called *shūren*. *Shūren* may be seen in the business world in the relationship between subordinate and boss, although in recent years the example of the boss who manages his subordinates harshly without any feedback has become rarer. That said, Westerners who have Japanese bosses are still often **puzzled by** the lack of feedback.

It is true that this lack of feedback is different from the communication and management style in the West.

技
わざ

　日本人が「修練」を重ねて、さまざまな技術を身につけ、自他共に人に教えることができるほどにそれを習得したとき、人々はその人が「技」を習得したといって敬意を表します。

　「技」を習得した人は、それでも常に「謙遜」しながら、さらに習得した「技」に**磨きをかけます**。「磨く」という日本語は、武士がその昔、常に手入れするために刀を磨いていたことからくる表現です。

　そして、「技を磨く」ことによって、単にその技術を高めるだけではなく、技術の習得を通じて、その人自身の精神性を向上させることが期待されるのです。したがって、「技」を教える人は、学ぶ人にあえて厳しい**質問や課題をだし**、それに耐えてゆける人格を育てようとするのです。教える人が学ぶ人の人生に口を差し挟み、あたかも親のように指導を行う中で、技を習得することにふさわしい人格形成を期待してゆくわけです。

　現在でも、会社の上司が部下の人生に**いろいろと世話をやき**、時には業務とは直接関係のない事柄でも指導しようとすることがあります。これも、「技」を習得するために、教える者が学ぶ者とどう接するかという伝統的な考え方からきているのです。

　「技」と英語でいう「スキル」との違いは、まさにそこにあるのかもしれません。「スキル」は、目的を達成させ結果を出すために必要な技術を指します。「技」に対して、より狭く、合理的な考え方が「スキル」であるといえそうです。

Skill

When a person repeats *shūren* to the extent that he is able to teach others, then it is said that he has truly mastered a *waza* ("skill") and he is given due respect for that.

After one has mastered a *waza*, one must continue to be modest and further "**polish**," *migaku*, one's skills. The word *migaku* in this case comes from the act of polishing a sword, when a samurai would polish his weapon many times over in order to bring out its best.

When a person "polishes his skills," he is not simply improving his technique; he may also expect to become stronger mentally and spiritually. Therefore the teacher will **pose** particularly difficult **questions and topics** to his student, seeking to toughen up the student in this way. The teacher will in a sense take on the role of a parent, going so far as to probe into the life of the student, and in this way hope to develop a well-rounded person as part of the process of mastering *waza*.

Even now, managers in companies will **get involved in** the personal lives of their subordinates, going so far on occasion as to give direction on matters not directly related to work. This comes from the traditional practice of how a teacher interacts with a student in order to master *waza*.

The difference between *waza* and its English translation, "skill," lies precisely here. A "skill" is mastered with a specific objective in mind. A "skill" is a narrower and more practical concept than that of a *waza*.

匠
たくみ

　最近、日本では伝統的な「技」をもって工芸や手仕事に携わる人が見直されてきています。こうした人々のことを「匠」と呼びます。

　「匠」は、長い年月をかけて「型」を習得し、そこからさらに「技」を磨いて、技能を極めた職人のことを意味しています。

　細かい手仕事など、人間にしかできない技術をもって伝統的な作品を作る職人は、機械化と**合理化**の中で次第に廃れてゆきました。しかし、最近の日本の伝統的な職人芸を**見直そう**という動きの中で、各所で「匠」の「技」が再発見されてきています。

　実は、自動車業界などの製造業においても、研磨など、人の勘や**微細な技量**が必要とされる分野で、「技」をいかに次世代に伝えてゆくか試行錯誤が繰り返されています。

　「匠」の「技」をいかに若い世代に伝えるかというとき、果たして伝統的な**師匠と弟子との関係**を今の若い世代が受け入れてゆけるのかという課題があるのです。師匠を常に尊敬し、文字通り人生を預けるようにして技術を磨くのか、それとも「スキル」として実用的な技術の習得に努めるのか。難しい選択といえましょう。

　特に、日本の伝統的な会社が、国際環境で海外の人を育成するとき、日本流の師弟関係は通用しません。時代に合った、「匠」の「技」の伝承が求められているのです。

Craft

Recently those involved in traditional handicrafts in Japan have come to be viewed in a new light. In Japanese, these people are said to have a *takumi* ("craft").

These craftsmen develop their *takumi* through many years of mastering a *kata* ("form"), followed by further polishing of their *waza* ("skill"). Such craftsmen, who create traditional items that can only be made by hand, have been dwindling in numbers in this age of continued industrialization and **rationalization**. However, as the products created by these craftsmen have been **reevaluated** in recent years, so also have the *takumi* these artisans possess.

In fact, in the automobile and other industries, efforts are being made through trial and error to pass on to the next generation grinding and other skills that require **detailed handiwork** and **intuition**.

In trying to pass on to the next generation various *takumi* and *waza*, there is the issue of whether or not younger people will accept the traditional **teacher-student relationship**. Will they respect their teacher, entrusting their lives to him as they polish their *waza*, or will they simply work to master a narrow skill? It is a difficult choice to make.

It is not possible to use this traditional teacher-student model when training people outside of Japan. In that case, a new model for *takumi* and *waza* must be used.

3

道

Way

道

　「型」が技術を学ぶための**具体的なノウハウ**であるとすれば、「道」は「型」を学び、その技量を高めてゆくための**精神的な価値観**を示す言葉です。

　「道」は「みち」と発音される場合と、中国語のdaoからの「どう」と発音される場合があります。「道」は英語のroadあるいはwayにあたり、人が歩き、車が通るところを指す言葉です。その「道」を人生に**なぞらえる**ことは、欧米でもよくあることです。そして、日本では、「型」の学習を「道」になぞらえて考えます。「道」は人がしなければならないことを示す言葉として、人生の色々な場面での処し方、道徳律を示す言葉としても使用されているのです。

　日本人は伝統的に「道」というコンセプトを好み、人としての生き方を語るときにこの言葉を使用します。たとえば、「人としての道をはずす」といえば、**不道徳な生き方をしている**ことを示します。また、「道を極める」といえば、匠の境地に至り、その分野の極意を極めた達人となることを意味します。

　したがって、日本人は、学習し、技を磨かなければならない事柄に「道」という言葉を頻繁に付加します。

　華道といえば、生け花を習得するプロセスを指し、剣道はもっと直裁に日本流のフェンシングとしてスポーツの名前になっています。柔道も同様ですし、日本古来の宗教も神道といわれ、この場合は「しんとう」と発音されます。

Way, Road

If *kata* is the **concrete know-how** by which a skill is learned, then *michi* is the **spiritual value** by which that skill is further strengthened.

The Chinese character for *michi* can also be read as *dō* (from the Chinese "dao"). In English, *michi* would be translated as "way" or "road," the path used by a person to walk or by a vehicle to travel. The same as in Japanese for *michi*, the words "way" or "road" are often used in Western languages as **metaphors** for life. In Japan, *michi* is also often used as a metaphor for the process of learning various *kata* as one proceeds down the road of life, doing what one must to become a more virtuous person.

The Japanese have traditionally liked the concept of *michi* and will often use it when describing the type of life led by a person. For example, if a person is **leading an immoral life**, they will say that that person is *fudōtoku* ("not on the road of virtue"). As another example, when a person pushes his skill to the utmost and is on the cutting edge of a field, the Japanese say that he is "**taking the road to its ultimate destination**" (*michi wo kiwameru*).

The word *michi* is therefore often used when the Japanese are describing circumstances where they must learn or polish a skill.

Kadō (written with the characters for "flower" and "way") is the art of flower arrangement; *kendō* ("sword" and "way") is the martial art of fencing; *jūdō* ("flexible" and "way") is another martial art; and *Shintō* ("gods" and "way"—here pronounced *tō*) is the native religion of Japan.

　「道」の考え方は、遠くに至るまで続く学習方法を示すことによって、そのhowに従って生きようとする日本人の文化背景に**根ざした**価値観であるといえましょう。

道理

　「道理」とは、ロジックを意味した言葉です。

　「道理」の「理」という言葉は、「ことわり」ともよみ、それは**物事の本来あるべき姿**を示す言葉です。また、ロジックにかなった当然の帰結をも意味する言葉です。その言葉に「道」の概念が加わり「道理」となるわけで、それは、人が道徳律に従った行動をし、ロジックもしっかりとしていることを指し示すときに使用されるのです。

　封建時代からずっと日本人が培ってきた価値観にそって、たとえば年上の人を敬い、師匠や上司に敬意を払って、それにふさわしい行動をすることは、日本では「**道理に叶った**」行動であるといわれます。

　すなわち、単に理屈が通り、ロジックに支えられているのではなく、そこにしっかりとした**道徳的なバックアップ**があることが「道理」の意味するところなのです。そして、その道徳は、日本の伝統的な価値観に支えられているわけで、必ずしも万国全てに受け入れられるものではありません。

　人生のあり方を示す「道」という価値観が、日本人のロジックの構成に大きく影響を与えている証拠が、この「道理」という言葉なのです。

The concept of *michi* reflects the approach taken to learning since ancient times in Japan; it is a social value **with deep roots in** Japanese culture.

Reason

The English translation for *dōri* would be "reason."

The Chinese character of *ri* in *dōri* is also read as *kotowari* and means the "**proper structure**" of things, or in other words, "reason" or "truth." By adding the character for *dō* ("way") to *ri*, we come up with *dōri*, or the proper "structure" of a person, with the concept of "reason" also clearly expressed.

In keeping with social values which have been cultivated since feudal times, the Japanese use the phrase *dōri ni kanatta* ("**following reason**") to describe the actions of a person who pays proper respect to his elders, teachers, or superiors.

In other words, it is not enough to simply put forth clever arguments; *dōri* requires that one must also have a **moral backbone** supporting one's words. As this morality is based on traditional values nurtured in Japan, it is not something that one can expect to be accepted in all countries around the world.

Proof that the social value of *michi,* or *dō*, is imbedded in the concept of reason can be seen in the very word *dōri*, which includes the character for *dō*.

武士道

　「道」という概念を最も端的に表しているのが、封建時代に武士が自らのあるべき生き方として心に刻んでいた「武士道」という価値観です。

　「武士道」については、明治時代の思想家であり外交官でもある新渡戸稲造が『武士道』という名著を残しています。

　新渡戸稲造は、ちょうど欧米でのキリスト教のように、それを日本人の道徳律の源泉であるとして、封建時代から培ってきた日本人の価値観、善悪を判断する基準としての道徳律が「武士道」であると説いているのです。

　武士のことを別のいい方で侍と呼び、そちらの方が欧米では有名になってしまいました。武士とは刀をもって戦い、時には主君や村や町を敵から守る人のことを指します。侍は、その武士が封建制度の枠組みにそって主君に仕えてゆく中で生まれた言葉です。

　ちょうど西欧の騎士のように、主君に対して忠誠を誓い、必要とあれば命も捧げて主君とその領土を守り抜くことが侍の勤めでした。そのために常に精神的、肉体的な鍛錬を怠らず、死をも克服できる強い人格形成に努めることが、侍のあるべき姿とされたのです。こうした侍の人生観と、それに育まれた行動様式が武士の「道」、すなわち「武士道」なのです。

　忠誠を貫くために常に何を学び、いかに振る舞うべきか。人の上に立つ身分である侍が常に心がけなければならない義務や掟はどのようなものか。「武士道」は、個人の欲望を抑え、質素な中で清廉に生き、死を畏れずに主君

The Way of the Warrior

The concept of *michi,* or *dō,* was **expressed in its purest form** by *bushi* ("warriors") during the feudal period in the way of life known as *bushidō.*

The Meiji Era (1868-1912) philosopher and diplomat Nitobe Inazo wrote a well-known book entitled *Bushidō: The Soul of Japan.*

In this book, Nitobe made the argument that *bushidō* is to Japan as Christianity is to the West, in the sense that *bushidō* is the **source of moral law** in Japan, providing the basis for judging right and wrong.

Another expression for *bushi* is *samurai*, a word that has become better known in the West. The *bushi* fought with swords, and at times could be called on to protect their masters or villages or towns from enemies. The *samurai* were *bushi* who, in the feudal structure of the time, served their lords.

As with the knights of the West, the *samurai* **swore allegiance to** their lords and were prepared to sacrifice their lives in defense of him and his land. To fulfill their role, the *samurai* trained hard both physically and mentally to develop a **fortitude** that could withstand the constant threat of death. This way of viewing life and the actions which grew out of such a view were the *dō* ("way") which the *bushi* traversed; hence the word *bushidō.*

In the **pursuit of loyalty**, the *bushi* were always concerned about what to learn and how to act. As persons of higher rank than others, what type of **responsibilities and rules** did the *samurai* in fact have to keep in mind? *Bushidō* taught the

を守り抜くことの大切さを教えていました。そして、侍は、寡黙で、物事に動じる事なく、**常に平常心で危急に対**処する精神力が求められたのです。

　現在でも日本には、個人の利益よりも会社の責務を優先し、だまって命ぜられた業務をこなすビジネスの環境が見受けられます。特に上に立つ者は、部下の過ちも自らの責任として引き受けようとすることを美徳とする風習が残っています。

　若い世代にこの「武士道」が廃れてきたと嘆く年配の人も多くいます。そして、もちろん、昔でも現実が「武士道」の**理想**と乖離したことも多々ありました。

　しかし、これからも日本人の価値観の一番奥底に、「武士道」的な発想が、時代によって変化しながらも、受け継がれていくのではないでしょうか。

克己心
こっきしん

　武士道で最も美徳とされる価値観に「克己心」があります。それは、**己に打ち勝つ心**という意味で、**精神修養**に努めることで、自らの欲望や恐怖を克服する精神的な高みを目指そうとする心がけを指す言葉です。
　日本人は伝統的に、努力という言葉を好みます。そして、往々にして、結果よりもそれに至るプロセスでの努力を重くみて、人を評価する傾向があります。それは、人が

importance of controlling individual desires, not fearing death, and leading a simple life of integrity as one protected one's lord. *Samurai* were also expected to be **taciturn**, unswayed by events around them, able to **remain calm** and respond to danger at any time.

In today's business world in Japan this way of thinking can still be found, as duty to one's company comes before individual profit, and company employees take care of requested assignments with few questions. It can also be seen in the case of managers who take responsibility for the mistakes of their subordinates.

Many older Japanese are disappointed that the younger generation has fallen away from the principles of *bushidō*. Of course, even in the past, the reality of *bushidō* was not always aligned with the **ideal**.

However, even as the times continue to change, it seems likely that *bushidō* will remain at the heart of Japanese social values.

Self-Denial

Within the tenets of *bushidō*, the most highly valued is the virtue of *kokkishin* ("self-denial"). *Kokkishin* means to conquer, through **spiritual training**, desire, fear, and other emotions in order to **overcome the self**.

The Japanese have traditionally liked the word *doryoku* ("effort"). There is a tendency to more highly value the effort put into the process than the result itself. This is a matter of how

いかに「克己心」をもって業務や学業に取り組んできたか
を重くみる、「武士道」的ものの考え方の名残りともいえ
ましょう。

　自分の欲望や利益をあえて横において、組織や集団の発
展のために力を注ぐことをよしとするこうした考え方に立
っていうならば、結果を示して人に自らの実力をアピール
することは、むしろよくないことであると考えられます。

　現代社会では、ビジネスにおいて常に**結果が求められま
す**。それは日本でも例外ではありません。しかし、しっか
りと努力する人間への同情や理解が、他の国々よりも深い
のも、また日本のビジネス文化の特徴といえそうです。

　こうした考え方は、「謙遜」や「謙虚」といった価値観に
も通じるもので、常に自らはへりくだって、黙々と努力を
重ねることが、「克己心」の意味するところなのです。

　寡黙に努力することをよしとする日本のビジネス文化
を、**自らの価値をしっかりとアピールし**、人に対してリー
ダーシップをとってゆくことを大切にする欧米の文化と
比較してみると、その違いがさまざまな誤解の原因になる
ことがわかってくるのです。

業
ぎょう

　「業」とは、直訳すればトレーニングということになる
のでしょうか。しかし、その意味するところは、「克己心」
を培うために日常的に**厳しい義務**を己に課してゆくこと
なのです。

much *bushidō*-like effort has been put into work or studies in the spirit of *kokkishin* ("self-denial").

It is often the case that those who put aside their own desires and benefits, working hard instead for the good of their organization or group, will be seen in more favorably than those who produce individual results.

Today's business world is **results-driven**. It is true that even in Japan there are no exceptions to this. That said, it is also true that in Japan's business culture, more so than in other countries, there is still more recognition and understanding of the value of effort for effort's sake.

In this way, *kokkishin* is related to the social value of *kenson* or *kenkyo* ("modesty"), where one constantly puts oneself below others and quietly strives to better oneself.

There are often misunderstandings between the Japanese business world, where taciturnity is valued, and the West, where people are expected to **speak up for themselves** and take the lead when necessary.

Training

If one must translate *gyō*, the closest word in English would probably be "training." However, this would be "training" in the sense of tasking oneself with the **demanding responsibility** of working hard day-to-day to cultivate one's *kokkishin* ("self-denial").

　それは、ちょうど僧侶が悟りを目指して行う修行に通じるものがあります。実際日本では、山奥の厳しい環境で修行をすることを、「業」を行うと表現します。

　「型」を学ぶときの「修練」も、ある意味では「業」であるといえましょう。以前、アメリカ人の著者、ロバート・ホワイティングが日本の野球を単なるスポーツとしてではなく、剣道や柔道と同じく、野球道であると評論しました。
　それは、日本人が野球の練習をするときに、ただ技能を磨くのではなく、野球場という自らを鍛える場への敬意を学ぶために行う清掃から、先輩への礼儀作法、さらに一見野球の技術とは関係のない禅寺での座禅まで、精神的な側面を極めて重くみるトレーニングを重ねていることを彼がみたからです。まさに、野球を極めるための「業」をしているのだと、ロバート・ホワイティングは思ったのでしょう。
　「業」という精神性を重んずる訓練の方法は、現在のビジネスでの新人研修にも多く取り入れられています。
　「業」は日本人のトレーニングに関する考え方の基本にある価値観で、何かを成し遂げるための長い「道」を進む上で大切な考え方なのです。

求道
（ぐどう）

　「業」を行い、自らが極めようとしている事柄に対して熱心に学習したり修行したりすることを「求道」と言います。

Buddhist priests do such training when they are seeking **enlightenment** (*satori*). In Japan, when one does such tough training deep in the mountains, one is said to be "**conducting gyō**" (*gyō wo okonau*).

The *shūren* ("discipline") used when one is learning *kata* ("forms") may be said to be a type of *gyō*. Robert Whiting, an American author, has written that Japanese baseball is in fact not a sport but rather a discipline, *yakyūdō*, along the same lines as *kendō* or *jūdō*.

He points out that Japanese players do not simply practice baseball; rather they also place emphasis on the spiritual side in their training—paying respect to the ball field by keeping it clean, being properly deferential to their seniors, and even going so far as to **sit in meditation** in *Zen* temples. It must have been very clear to Whiting that the players were employing a particularly Japanese form of training, *gyō*, in order to reach the top of their game.

In today's business world, many aspects of *gyō* are also used in the mental or spiritual training of workers.

For the Japanese, *gyō* is an essential value in all training; it is an important aspect of the *michi* ("road") one travels in seeking to accomplish anything.

Seeking the Truth

When one trains and studies hard to thoroughly master something, this is called *gudō* ("seeking the truth").

　「道」を極めるために、しっかり修行し、自らを律する行為が「業」であるならば、そうした「業」を真摯に行う心がけが「求道」の精神です。

　「道」という価値観を重んずる日本人は、「道」を極めるためにいかに努力し、目標に向けて「修練」を重ねるかということに強い関心を示します。「克己心」の項目でも紹介しましたが、「道」を極めるためのこうしたプロセスへの美学がそこに見受けられます。

　仮に結果が思わしくなくても、そこに至るプロセスにおいて努力を重ねていれば、人はそれを評価し尊敬します。「求道」の精神こそが、結果以上に求められているのです。

　ある意味で、結果重視の欧米型のビジネス文化からみるならば、「求道」の精神やプロセスを重んずる日本人の行動様式は**非合理的**にみえるかもしれません。

　しかし、日本人からみるならば、結果を得ることそのものよりも、努力することで得られる経験や精神的な高みのほうがより重要なのです。

　その経験が培った強い精神力があれば、たとえそこでの結果が思わしくないとしても、他の「場」において、しっかりと物事に取り組むことができるというわけです。

　武士道においても、もしその人が精神鍛錬をしっかりと行えば、**結果は自ずとついてくる**と教えられます。

　試合に勝つことは、訓練を重ねてきたことの、一つの結果に過ぎないというわけです。

If one defines *gyō* as the act of doing such training in order to find one's way (*michi*), then one can think of *gudō* as the sincere spirit employed in doing one's *gyō*.

For the Japanese, who highly value the concept of *michi,* there is a strong interest in how one disciplines oneself as one works hard to find one's way and reach a goal. As touched upon in the section on *kokkishin* ("self-denial"), one can see the **aesthetic** of seeking one's way in the process itself.

Even if the results are not what were hoped for, people will positively judge the effort made in the process. It is precisely in the spirit of *gudō* that something more than simply results is expected.

From the perspective of Westerners, who place a heavy emphasis on results in their business culture, the spirit of *gudō*, with the importance placed on the process, must seem **impractical**.

However, from the Japanese perspective, the experience and the improvement in one's spirit gained through the effort are more important than the results.

Even if the results are not good in a particular situation, one will be able to better handle future situations, thanks to the stronger spirit that one has developed.

In *bushidō*, it was thought that if one trained properly to develop the proper spiritual power, then **the results would take care of themselves**.

In other words, coming out ahead in a competition is nothing more than one result of the training that has been done.

4

気

Energy

気

気

気は英語でも*Qi*あ
るいは*Ki*として、そ
のまま使用される
ケースもある。そ
の場合、気は"生命"
に直結しており、
Energy に近い意味
のことが多い。

「気」とは古代中国に生まれた概念で、この世にある**目には見えないエネルギーの動き**を意味します。

たとえば、会議をしているとき、お互いに意見が対立して、何も前に進まなかったとしましょう。そのとき、会議室の中になんとなく**鬱々とした雰囲気**が漂います。その雰囲気も「気」の一つです。

朝、澄んだ空気の中を歩いていると心が爽快になります。そんな気持ちを呼び起こす雰囲気も「気」なのです。

すなわち、「気」がよければ人は前向きで元気になり、「気」が悪ければ人は精神的にも肉体的にもくたびれてしまいます。

「気」の概念は古代の日本に伝わり、今でも日本人のものの考え方や判断のしかたに**大きな影響を与えて**います。

「気」は場所や時間、あるいは人との関係やコミュニケーションの状況などによってさまざまに変化します。そして、「気」は人の心の中にもあり、その人の中によい「気」が充満していれば、仕事にも個人の生活にも**充実感がある**はずだと日本人は思うのです。

また、多くの場合「気」は、自分の努力で変えることができるのです。たとえば「気」が悪いと意識したら、それをよくするために何をすべきか人は考えます。会議でよい結論がでず、行き詰まったとき、休憩をとって気分転換をはかるのも、「気」を変えてよい**エネルギーを呼び込む**手段といえましょう。

Energy

Ki, which is a concept developed in ancient China, describes the movement of **unseen** energy in our world.

For example, let's say that in a meeting there is a difference of opinion that prevents the discussion from moving forward. In that situation, a **depressed atmosphere** will envelop the conference room. That atmosphere is an example of one type of *ki*.

When one walks in a morning's clear air, one feels refreshed. The feelings brought forth in that case are an example of another type of *ki*.

In other words, if one encounters good *ki*, one feels energetic and positive, while if one encounters bad *ki*, one feels poorly and lacks energy both spiritually and physically.

Ki has been a concept in Japan since ancient times, and today it still **has a large influence on** how the Japanese think and view things.

Ki will change depending on the time and place, as well as the kind of relationship of the people involved and the circumstances of their communication. *Ki* is also found in people's hearts, and the Japanese believe that if a person is full of good *ki*, then he will **be fulfilled** in both his work and his personal life.

In most cases, one should be able to change one's *ki* through one's own efforts. For example, if one feels that one's *ki* is not good, then one should consider in concrete terms how to improve one's *ki*. If a meeting is not progressing well, then one might consider taking a break to change the atmosphere and **generate better energy**.

「気」を読み取って、うまく対処できる人間が、より評価されるのです。「配慮」の項で紹介した「気配り」という概念は、まさにその時の「気」を理解して、相手に対する対応を考えることなのです。

それはロジックではありません。それゆえに文化背景の違う欧米の人にとって、「気」の概念を理解することは大変なことかも知れません。

やる気

「気」という漢字は、さまざまな熟語や単語の中に組み込まれて使われます。「やる気」もその一つで、これは人が何か自らがやりたいことを成し遂げようと積極的に取り組む意識を指す言葉です。すなわち、「やる気」とは、**新しい環境に対して前向きに取り組む「気」をもっている**ことを示すのです。

会社に入社したり、学校でクラブ活動に加わったりしたとき、人が自らの積極性を示そうとすることは、どこでもみかけることです。

日本の場合、「やる気」を示すには、自分の能力をアピールするのではなく、自らが加わる集団にいかに積極的にとけ込もうとしているかを見せてゆかなくてはなりません。

たとえば、新入社員はまず誰よりも早く出社して、オフィスの掃除をしたりする行動こそが、最も適切な「やる気」の示し方です。中学校や高校のスポーツクラブなどに新入生が入ったときも同様です。野球部であれば、新しく入った者は、野球をするのではなく、バットを磨き、ボー

People who are capable of **gauging** *ki* and handling it in an appropriate way are highly thought of. In the section on *hairyo* ("consideration"), we discussed the concept of *kikubari* ("sharing one's heart"). This is indeed a case of understanding the *ki* of the moment and being attuned to the needs of other people.

The concept of *ki* is not necessarily logical. For Westerners, who have grown up with a different culture, *ki* may indeed be a foreign concept.

Will to Do

The Chinese character for *ki* is used in combination with many other characters to form a variety of words and phrases. One example would be *yaru ki*, which means having the will to do something. More specifically, *yaru ki* implies having the *ki* ("will") to **take on a difficult challenge in a new environment**.

It is common everywhere to see people taking on new challenges, such as joining a company or participating in a club at school.

In the case of people in Japan, to show their *yaru ki*, it is necessary when joining a new group to not boast about one's abilities and instead to make every effort to fit in.

A very good example of *yaru ki* would be the new person in a company getting to work before anyone else and doing such things as cleaning up around the office. It would be the same for someone joining a sports club in middle school or high school. In the case of a baseball club, rather than playing baseball, the

ルをそろえ、フィールドを整えることによって、その集団に自分が**貢献している**ことを示すのです。

　「やる気」をうまく示すことのできる人は、集団により暖かく迎えられるのです。

気概

　「やる気」が、**新参者**に求められる意識であれば、「気概」はその「やる気」を継続しようという強い意識のことです。

　第6章で説明する「情」の概念でも触れますが、日本では「やる気」や「気概」を示すことによって上の立場の者や同僚から好かれることが、実際によい実績を示すことより重要視される場合が多くあります。

　たとえ、結果が思わしくない場合でも、その人物に「気概」があり、集団によい「気」を与えることができるほうが、**高く評価される**のです。

　「やる気」を示す、あるいは「気概」を示す行為がない場合、いかに仕事ができても、いわゆるアウトローとして扱われ、集団の中での昇進にはつながらないかもしれません。

　これは、グループ行動を一義とする日本社会の特徴といえるのではないでしょうか。

　また、「気」がロジックではなく、あくまでも雰囲気を伝えることからもわかるように、「気概」を示す行為は、何らビジネス上のロジックには結びつきません。それは単に**熱心さを示す**ことに過ぎないといえばその通りです。しかし、熱心であることは、グループや組織に対して愛情があり、忠誠心があることを意味します。自らのパフォーマンスのみを強調するよりも、全員が同じ「気概」をもっ

new person would **make his contribution** by polishing the bats, picking up balls, and getting the field in shape.

A person who dose a good job of showing his *yaru ki* will be warmly welcomed to the new group.

Fighting Spirit

If *yaru ki* is the will expected of a **new participant in a group**, then *kigai* is the strong continued daily expression of that will.

In Chapter 6 we will discuss the concept of *jō*, where we will note that rather than results, it is common in Japan to more highly value the praise of superiors and colleagues earned through one's *yaru ki* or *kigai*.

Even if the results are not good, if one has *kigai* and is able to contribute good *ki* to the group, then one will be **favorably evaluated**.

If a person does not show sufficient *yaru ki* or *kigai*, then no matter how well he does his work, that person will be treated as an "outlaw" and he may not be promoted within the group.

This may be one of the reasons why group action is such a strong component of Japanese society.

In the same way that *ki* is based on atmosphere, not logic, there is also no connection between *kigai* and business logic. If one wishes to say that this is simply a matter of **expressing enthusiasm**, one would have to agree that this is so. However, having enthusiasm is also an expression of love and loyalty to one's group or organization. Most Japanese believe that the power of the group created by pulling together the *kigai* of

て業務に取り組んだほうが、よりよい結果を出せると、多くの日本人は信じているのです。

気持ち

「気持ち」とは、人の思いや感情を示す一般的な言葉です。

しかし、この言葉にはもう一つの意味があります。それは、人に対する「気配り」です。

たとえば、お鮨屋さんに行ったとします。鮨を握る職人さんと会話がはずみ、最後に注文していない鮨が振る舞われたとき、職人さんは、「これは私の気持ちです」と言います。この場合、その鮨は無料で、職人さんの特別なサービスであることを意味しているのです。

お世話になっている人に対して、自らの**感謝**の意思を示すことが「気持ち」なのです。会社の同僚や友人などに対して、彼らがどのようにして欲しいか考えて、本人よりも先に対応するのも「気持ち」の現れです。

日本人は「和」や「遠慮」の概念を大切にするあまり、自らのニーズを先に主張することはほとんどありません。

それだけに、相手のニーズを察知して時には先回りして対応することが求められます。

言葉を換えれば、相手の「気」を読んで、相手が安心したり喜ぶように対応しなければならないのです。そうした心づもりが「気持ち」なのです。

他民族国家で、さまざまな文化背景が混在する社会では、相手のニーズを言葉以外から察知することは困難です。

「私の気持ちです（無料です）」を英語で表現すれば、"compliment"となる。元々の意味は、相手を褒めたり、ちょっとしたお世辞をいうことで、その延長でお世話になった顧客に無料のサービスをするときに使うこともある。

everyone will produce better results than relying on individual performance.

Feelings

The word *kimochi* is commonly used to mean the thoughts and feelings expressed by people.

However, this word has one more meaning. This is the sense of *kikubari* ("sharing of the heart").

For example, let's say that one goes to a sushi shop. At the end of the meal an additional piece of sushi that had not been ordered is put out by the chef, who says, "This is an expression of my feelings (*kimochi*)." In this case, the chef is providing special service and there will be no charge for the additional piece.

Gratitude to those who have done us favors is an expression of one's *kimochi*. Understanding the desires of one's colleagues or friends and fulfilling those desires before being asked is another example of expressing *kimochi*.

Because *wa* ("harmony") and *enryo* ("reserve") are so important, it is rare that a Japanese person will insist on putting his own needs first.

That is why it is expected that the needs of other people will be understood and taken care of first.

In other words, one must read the *ki* of the other person and then do what one can to satisfy that person. This is known as expressing *kimochi*.

In other countries where there are many different cultures living together, it is often difficult to express one's needs without

そうした社会では、自分が何を欲するかをしっかりと相手に伝えることからコミュニケーションがはじまります。

　それに対して、同じ文化背景をもった人が集まる日本では、ニーズは無言でも相手に伝わりやすく、それゆえに「気持ち」をもって**先手を打つ**ことが可能となるのです。

気丈

　「気丈」とは悲しいとき、動揺しているときに自らをコントロールする強い意志を示す言葉です。

　2011年の東日本大震災で、その惨状が世界に報道されたとき、ある外国の人が日本人は本当に悲しんでいるのだろうかと質問しました。外国でみられるように、大声で叫んだり泣いたりしている光景がみられず、日本人が控えめなことが不思議だったのでしょう。

　日本人は、人前で強く感情を表すことを嫌います。感情をあらわにすることは、何よりも「和」を乱す行為とされます。同じ悲しみを抱く他の人への「配慮」にも欠ける行為だと思うのです。すなわち日本には「気丈」であることをよしとする文化背景があるのです。

　もちろん、日本人にも感情があり、今回の大震災で愛する肉親を失った人々の悲しみは深いはずです。しかし、その悲しみの感情をどう表現するかが多くの国と異なるのです。

　よく日本人は何を考えているのかわからないといわれます。第6章で紹介する「本音と建前」といったような日

words. In those societies, communication begins only after one has clearly expressed one's desires in words.

In contrast, it is easier for the Japanese, who all possess a common culture and background, to express needs even without words, allowing them to express their *kimochi* by **acting before being asked**.

Tough-minded

Kijō means controlling one's emotions, even when faced with a very sad or disturbing situation.

At the time of the Great Eastern Japan Quake of 2011, there were reports of people overseas asking if the Japanese were really saddened by the event. For people overseas, who are used to seeing scenes of crying and screaming in such situations, the reserve of the Japanese must have been surprising.

The Japanese do not like to show emotion in front of other people. More than anything, it is felt that such behavior does not show concern (*hairyo*) for others who are dealing with similarly sad emotions and that the *wa* ("harmony") of the situation will be disrupted. In other words, this is a culture where it is all right to be "tough-minded" (*kijō*).

Of course the Japanese also do have emotions, and the grief of those who lost loved ones in the earthquake and tsunami must be deep indeed. However, the way in which that emotion is expressed is different from that of many other countries.

It is often said by non-Japanese that they have a difficult time knowing what the Japanese are thinking. It is true that such

本人ならではのコミュニケーションスタイルが、そうした戸惑いの原因となっていることもあるでしょう。それに加え、ここで語っているように、感情を表情や言葉にして表に出さない**国民性**も、こうした疑問へとつながっているはずです。

「気丈」とは、決して心が冷たいことを意味しません。

「気丈」である人ほど、悲しみに必死で耐えているわけで、それは日本人には容易に理解できることなのです。さらにいうならば、日本人にとっては、「気丈」な人であれば、かえって同情が集まるのです。

運気

「運気」とは、いわゆる**占い**の世界での運勢の動きを示す言葉です。西欧の**占星術**と同じように、中国や韓国、そして日本でも、星の動きやその人の生年月日、名前などを組み合わせた複雑な解析方法による占いが昔から存在します。

日本人は占いが好きで、テレビのワイドショーでは今日の運勢を占うコーナーがあり、繁華街には占い師がいて、**手相**や**姓名判断**などをみてもらおうと多くの人がやってきます。

「運気」は「気」の動きと深く関わっています。「気」の悪い状態におかれれば、その人の「運気」は下がり、やがて病気や何かの**トラブルに巻き込まれる**といわれています。

「気」とは見えないエネルギーですが、それは個人の中にもあれば、宇宙の動きにも関連しています。「運気」の

concepts of communication as *honne* and *tatemae* ("true feelings" and "facade"), which will be discussed in Chapter 6, may be the source of such bewilderment. The additional **national trait**, discussed here, of a reluctance to express emotions or to put things into words, must also contribute to this problem.

Kijō does not imply that one is cold-hearted.

It is easy for a Japanese to understand that the more *kijō* ("tough-minded") a person is, the deeper his grief is. In fact, it can be said that the more *kijō* a person is, the more sympathy will be felt for him.

Fate

The word *unki* refers to the practice of **fortune telling**. Like the **astrology** of the West, a method of predicting one's fate based on a complex analysis of the stars or one's birthdate or name has existed in China, Korea, and Japan since ancient times.

Fortune telling is popular in Japan, with many people watching featured sections on TV shows or going to street stalls in the cities for **palm reading** and **analysis of names**.

Unki has a strong connection with the movement of *ki*. When the *ki* is not good, one's *unki* will be in a downward trend, and it is at such times that it is easy to become sick or **run into trouble** of some sort.

Ki is an energy that can not be seen, existing in individuals and also in connection with the movement of the universe.

強い人は、そうした「気」を前向きに取り込み、自らの気力を高め、強運を導き入れることができるというわけです。

日本には「病は気から」という言葉があります。この「気」はここで紹介する「気」のほかに、人の気持ちを示す「気」でもあるのです。つまり、精神状態がよくないと病の原因となるというのが、この言葉の意味するところです。

心の持ち方によって、人はさまざまな「気」を外に発することができます。したがって、前向きに物事を考えれば、自ずと病を克服し、強い運を呼び寄せることができるというわけです。

「運気」は自らの心の持ち方で大きく左右されるのです。

殺気

「気」の概念を理解するのに「殺気」は最適な概念かも知れません。

その昔、よく訓練された武士が**殺意をもった相手**に出会うと、相手が**刀を抜いて**挑みかかる前に、その殺意を感じることができたといわれていました。その殺意が空気のように漂っていることを「殺気」というのです。すなわち、言葉や明快な行動に表さなくても、そこで醸し出される雰囲気や、**微妙な表情や仕草**から、その人の発する「気」を読み取ることができるのです。

すでに何度か言及していますが、日本人は言葉の外にある意味を読んでコミュニケーションしようと試みます。昔、

People with a strong fate are those who are able to take hold of that *ki* and through their own efforts pull that energy into their lives.

In Japanese the word for illness (*byōki*) is made up of the Chinese characters for "sick" (*byō*) and *ki*. In addition to the meaning of *ki* introduced here ("energy"), *ki* can also mean "feelings," as in the *ki* of *kimochi*. In other words, one's poor emotional condition may become a cause of illness.

Depending on one's emotional state, one will emit various types of *ki*. If one is in a positive state of mind, one may be able to overcome an illness on one's own and bring good luck to oneself.

One's *unki* can change significantly depending on one's attitude.

Sensing Danger

Sakki is another concept that is helpful to know in order to understand the concept of *ki*.

In the old days, it was said that a well trained samurai could sense the **intent of someone to make an attempt on his life** even before his opponent had **drawn his sword**. That sense in the air is what is known as *sakki* ("sensing danger"). In other words, even without words or clear actions, the atmosphere and **subtle facial expressions or movements** would allow the well trained samurai to read the *ki* of his opponent.

As we have already explained a number of times, the Japanese will try to communicate in ways other than through

修行を重ねた武士は、相手が険しい表情をしたり、睨みつけたりという仕草をしていなくても、その人から「殺気」を感じ、心の中で闘う準備をしていたといわれています。

人の**発する**「気」は、相手に伝わり、相手はそれに対応して身構えることによって、自らの意思を無言で相手に伝えます。すなわち、「気」を交換することで、相対するふたりは互いに意思を伝達するのです。

現代社会において、これは漫画や映画の世界でのことですが、日本人は今でも言葉にして出すことなく、相手に気持ちを伝えようと期待することは事実です。ですから、外国の人からみれば、日本人が本当は何が言いたいのかよくわからないという戸惑いが生まれてしまうのです。

空気

「空気」は単に気体のことだけを意味しません。英語でも、「空気」は雰囲気などを示すときに使われる言葉です。

そして、日本語の場合も「空気を読む」という言葉があるように、人がコミュニケーションをするにあたって、そこでの雰囲気や様子が醸し出す状況を「空気」という言葉で表現します。

「空気」の「空」は、何もない**からっぽな状態**を示す漢字です。そのからっぽな状態に「気」が混ざり、「空気」となるのです。**言葉を換えれば**、「空気」は単なる気体ではなく、そこに**充満する**さまざまなエネルギーをすべて包括したものということになります。

words. Even if his opponent were not glaring at him with a severe expression, the well-trained samurai would "sense danger" and make his mental preparations for a fight.

The *ki* one **emits** is sent to the person one is with, and that person in turn readies himself so that one can now send his message to the other person without using words. In other words, by exchanging *ki*, two people are able to express their wills to each other.

In the modern world, this would be the stuff of comics or movies, but it is a fact that even now the Japanese expect to be able to express their feelings to others without using words. It is because of this that non-Japanese people are puzzled and have a difficult time trying to understand what the Japanese are saying.

Air, Atmosphere

Kūki ("air") is not simply a physical phenomenon. In English as well, "air" is also used to describe the atmosphere of a situation.

As in the Japanese phrase *kūki wo yomu* ("reading the air"), the conditions that have brought about a particular atmosphere or situation are said to be the *kūki*.

The Chinese character of *kū* in *kūki* is the character for "sky" and also means "**empty**." The character for *ki* is combined with the character for "sky" or "empty," to form *kūki*, or "air." **Putting it another way**, *kūki* is not merely a physical phenomenon; it also includes all of the various energies that **inundate** a particular situation.

気

そこに充満しているのが、どのような「気」なのかを察知し、それをもとに適切に物事に対処することは、日本人が常に心掛けている**処世術**ともいえましょう。

したがって、「空気」の概念は、第1章で紹介した「場」とも関連します。人と人が**集まる**タイミングや組み合わせによって、その場その場でさまざまな雰囲気が生まれます。すなわち、「場」に充満する空気を読み、たとえば話したい話題を予定通りに話すのか、それとも控えるのかといった判断をすることが、コミュニケーション上大切な戦略となるのです。

「気」は人と人とが**交流**する中で生み出されるエネルギーです。したがって、「場」や人の立場などを理解し、よりよい「気」をつくろうと多くの日本人は考えているのです。

「空気」は「場」のみならず「間」とも関連する。「間の悪い人だ」は、タイミングの悪い人という意味もあり、「間」の考え方がわからない人は、「空気を読めない人」ということにもなる。

As part of **getting along in life**, the Japanese will always try to determine what particular energies (*ki*) are coming to play in a situation and do their best to take appropriate action based on that.

The concept of *kūki* is therefore related to the concept of *ba* ("place") introduced in Chapter 1. Depending on the timing and combinations of when and where people **get together**, various types of atmosphere will be created. For example, as part of one's communication strategy, it is important to decide whether or not to bring up a particular subject based on the *kūki* of that *ba* ("place").

Ki is the energy that is created by the **intcrchange** between people. Therefore, most Japanese feel that it is important to do their best in understanding the circumstances of the people around them in order to create good *ki*.

5

節

Period

節

節と節目

"Milestones"は 道路の脇に置かれ、目的地までの距離を表示する標識のことで、昔は石に刻まれていたことからマイルストーンという。この言葉は、人生の中で大きな変化やイベントが起きたときのことも意味し、「人生の節目」を表現する言葉ともいえる。

「型」や「道」という価値を**重んずる**日本人は、常に自らがどの位置にあるかを知るためのマイルストーンを大切にします。このマイルストーンを表す言葉が「節」なのです。「節」は「せつ」とも「ふし」とも読みます。

「節」とは「節目」のことで、一年の「ふしめ」である四季のことを「節」の文字を使って季節と呼んだり、人生の大きな**転換期**を、人生の「節目」という風に表現します。

「節目」には始まりと終わりがあります。節のコンセプトを知るために、竹をイメージしてみてください。竹には「節」があり、その成長した節が重なって、一本の竹となっています。その一本の竹を人生、あるいは何かを学ぶプロセスと考えてみると、それぞれの「節」がいかに大切で、一つ一つの「節」がなければ竹は上に伸びないことが理解できるでしょう。

「道」を極めるにあたって、この「節」の**連続性**がいかに保たれ、一つずつの「節」の始まりと終わりをしっかりと意識し、次の「節」につなげるかが、物事を学び、人生を送る基本であるという価値観が「節目」には込められているのです。

「節目」を重んずる日本人が、変化するときに単に未来に向かわずに、それまでお世話になった人に敬意を表したり、しっかりと挨拶をしたりすることは、欧米に人からみると、時には**儀式ばって**みえるかもしれません。しかし、竹の解説からもおわかりのように、下の「節」を大切にしない限り、竹は上の「節」をつくり、伸びていかないのです。

*node [名] (竹などの)節

Period

For the Japanese, who **place much weight** on the values of *kata* ("form") and *michi* ("way"), it is important to always take note of milestones. In Japanese, the Chinese character *setsu*, also read as *fushi*, expresses this concept of milestone.

The character of *setsu* is used with the *ki* of *shiki* ("four seasons") to make the word *kisetsu* ("season"). Again, the same character, this time read as *fushi*, is used in the word *fushime* to indicate an important **transition point** in a person's life.

A *fushime* ("period") has a beginning and an end. Let's use the image of bamboo to help us better understand the concept of *fushi*. A bamboo stalk has *fushi* ("nodes"*), and the growth from node to node is what eventually results in a fully grown stalk. It is the same with one's life or with the process of learning something: each period is important and builds on the previous period; one cannot proceed to the next period without the last.

When seeking to master something, it is critical that **continuity** be preserved and that the beginning and end of each period be consciously recognized and connected with the next period, as part of the basic values of one's life. This is inherent in the concept of *fushime*.

From the point of view of Westerners, it must sometimes seem that the Japanese are simply **enacting superfluous ceremonies** when they mark the end of a period by going to the trouble of making various greetings and thanking people, rather than just moving on. But for the Japanese it is a matter, of making sure that the last *fushi* is properly taken care of, like the bamboo, in order to ensure the growth of the next.

　次の始まりに向かうためにも、過去をしっかりと見つめ直すということが、「節」という概念が示す倫理観なのです。

有終

　「有終」とは終わりをしっかりと意識するという価値観です。多くの場合、「節」あるいは「節目」に示される倫理観を最も端的に表した言葉が、「**有終の美**」です。

　たとえば、会社を辞めて、次のチャンスに向けて旅立つとき、人はまさに「節目」を経験します。その「節目」を大切にして、未来へ向かうために、辞めていく会社で最後の日までしっかりと働きます。そしてお世話になった人への挨拶を忘れず、**後任に引き継ぎをして**、時には自分の机や周囲の掃除までして会社を去ることが、「有終の美」の価値観なのです。

　この考え方は日常生活でもみることができます。ホテルや旅館に宿泊したとき、旅立つ前に部屋や布団を簡単に**片付け**たりする行為も「有終の美」の一例です。

　「**立つ鳥跡を濁さず**」ということわざがあります。これは、水鳥は飛び立つとき池を濁すことなくきれいに飛び立つという意味から、旅立つとき、またはその場を去るとき、後の人のためにもその場所を美しく保って去ってゆこうということを意味します。

　「有終の美」は、このことわざにもつながる、過去から未来への人や社会の繋がりをしっかりと意識するための倫理観といえるのではないでしょうか。

The ethics of *fushi* are clearly evident in this act of carefully considering what has happened in the past before moving on to something new.

Beautiful Ending

The word *yūshū* expresses the social value of coming to terms with an ending. In many cases, the ethical values of *fushi* or *fushime* can be expressed most directly in the phrase *yūshū no bi* ("**beautiful ending**").

For example, when a person quits his job and moves on to his next opportunity, he is clearly experiencing a *fushime* ("transition point"). "A beautiful ending" can be seen in this case, as the person treats the transition with respect, working hard up through the last day, making proper greetings to his colleagues, **briefing his replacement**, and even in the way he cleans out his desk before leaving his job.

We can also see this way of thinking in everyday life. Tidying up the room and **putting** the futon **away** before leaving a hotel or Japanese inn would be another example of a "beautiful ending."

There is a saying in Japan that "**a bird taking off doesn't muddy the waters.**" In the same way that a water bird takes flight from a pond without disturbing the water, so should a person, be careful to put things in order so as not to inconvenience those left behind.

The ethical sense behind a "beautiful ending" is also seen in this saying, as one properly connects the people and events of one's past with one's future.

節度

　竹の「節」の一つ一つを人生になぞらえ、大切に生きてゆこうという発想は、自らが現在留まっている「節」の中で、自分を整え、その「節」を破ることなく、次の「節」に旅立つまでしっかりと「謙虚」に自分を磨こうという価値観を導きます。その価値観を「節度」と呼びます。「和」の章でみてきた、「謙遜」や「謙譲」、そして「謙虚」という価値観が融合して「節度」という意識となってここで活きてくるのです。

　あえて自らを強くアピールすることなく、現在おかれている位置や立場を理解し、その日々の積み重ねから自身が成長してゆくことが「節度」という価値観です。

　ダイナミックに変化する現代において、封建時代から培われてきたこの価値観は時代にそぐわないかもしれません。

　よく、日本人は何を考え、何がしたいのかわからないという苦情を（外国の人から）聞きますが、その背景には、日本人が常に「節度」という価値観を持ち、自らの考えや思いを強く主張することを控えようという意識があるからかもしれません。

　しかし、「節度」という価値観のよい面は、常に人に対して感謝や尊敬の念をもって接する心構えでしょう。

　現代のビジネス社会において、いかにチームワークをもってプロジェクトを進めてゆくかというテーマは大切です。そのとき、相手の立場を考え、相手に敬意を表しながら「節度」あるアプローチをとれば、多くの場合、対立がシナジーへと変化するかもしれません。

* **norm** [名] ①標準的な状態　②規範

Restraint

Just as each node in a bamboo stalk is like each period in one's life, so it is that one must also do the utmost to train and prepare oneself while one is in a particular period of life, while also being careful not to go on to the next stage before one is ready. This value is called *setsudo* ("restraint"). In the chapter on *wa* ("harmony"), we discussed the value of modesty (*kenson, kenjō, kenkyo*), and here we will see how modesty is reflected in the concept of *setsudo*.

Rather than seeking individual recognition, *setsudo* means working hard day-to-day to improve oneself within one's current position and situation.

This value, which has been cultivated in Japan since feudal times, may not fit with today's world, in which dynamic change is the norm*.

Non-Japanese may often complain that they don't know what the Japanese are thinking or what they want to do. *Setsudo* may be behind this, as the Japanese will refrain from giving strong opinions with this value in mind.

On the other hand, the good aspects of *setsudo* are the gratitude and respect always paid to other people.

In today's business world, the amount of teamwork that can be brought to bear on a project is very important. If an approach employing *setsudo* is used, one in which the position of other people is carefully considered and the proper respect is paid to them, then in a surprisingly large number of cases it may be possible to change conflict into synergy.

　価値観は古くなるのでも、的はずれになるのでもありません。むしろ、価値観にとらわれ形骸化した行動が、価値観そのものを古くさくしてしまうのです。

　そうした意味では、「節度」という価値観のよい面を見直してみるのも、必要なのではないでしょうか。

けじめ

　「有終の美」の概念でもおわかりのように、日本人は一見非合理的にすら見えるほどに、物事の終わりを大切にし、「節目」をしっかりと意識しながら未来へ向かうことをよしとします。

　この物事の変化にあたって、しっかりと「節」の価値観に従って行動することを日本人は「けじめ」といいます。

　たとえば、人が罪を犯した場合、ただ逃げ隠れするのではなく、あえて警察に自首し、刑に服することがあります。この行為を日本では、「けじめ」をつけるといいます。すなわち、自らの行動に対してしっかりと責任をとり、それにふさわしい態度や対応をすることが「けじめ」なのです。

　現在でも、日本人は「けじめ」を常に意識しているようです。

　たとえば、ビジネスの世界で、会社が不良品を製造したり、業績が低迷したりという厳しい状態におかれたとき、日本では会社の経営者が責任をとって辞任することが頻繁にあります。直接その人が原因で起きた問題でなくとも、責任者として、会社が未来へ向かうための「けじめ」をつけるのです。物事が変化する節目に、いかに「けじめ」をつけるか。日本人はそこでの行動に注目して、その人物

伝統的な価値観に従えば、辞任するだけではなく、個人的なリスクをも投げ打って責任を全うすることで「けじめ」であり、そうした意味では、「有終の美」と「けじめ」は関係の深い価値観と」いえる。

*incumbent［形］
現職の

It is not a matter of values becoming old and irrelevant on their own. Rather, it is a matter of the essence of values being lost due to the changing attitudes and actions of people.

In that sense, it may be necessary to acknowledge once again the good aspects of *setsudo*.

Marking a Break

As seen in the concept of *yūshū no bi* ("a beautiful ending"), the Japanese can appear impractical in how they treat endings, **taking due note of** *fushime* ("transition points") before moving on to a new stage of life.

Kejime is the action one takes **in accord with** the concept of *fushi* ("period") as one marks a change in one's life.

For example, if one commits a crime and, instead of running away, one **turns oneself into the police** and submits to the appropriate punishment, in Japan this is called *kejime wo tsukeru* ("marking a break"). In other words, having the right attitude to take responsibility for one's actions is an important aspect of *kejime*.

The Japanese today remain very aware of the concept of *kejime*.

For example, it is quite common in Japan for the chief executive of a company to **resign** if his company has manufactured and sold defective goods. Even if the executive was not the direct cause of the defective goods, as the head of the company, it is incumbent* on him to "mark a break" (*kejime wo tsukeru*) and take responsibility. For the Japanese, a person will be judged on how sincerely he "marks the break" during such a transition

を評価するわけです。

節約

　「節度」という概念を経済の上に投影したのが「節約」という考え方です。

　「節約」とは、単純に無駄遣いをせず、**質素に生きてゆく**ことの美学を示し、具体的にどのように無駄を削るかというノウハウを指す言葉です。

　「**もったいない**」という日本語が一時国連などでもてはやされたことがありました。これは資源を大切にするために、物を最後までしっかりと使おうという意味の言葉です。たとえばお風呂で使う石けんが小さくなったとします。すると、小さくなった石鹸をネットの袋にいれ、次の石鹸が小さくなった時も同じ袋に保存します。やがて、ネットの中は小さな石鹸でいっぱいになり、それで体を洗えば、石鹸を無駄にすることなく、スポンジを新たに買う必要もありません。小さい石鹸を捨てる行為を「もったいない」といって戒め、ネットの袋に石鹸を集めて使用する行為を「節約する」というわけです。

　質素と**倹約**は、「節約」という行為の２つの大きな要素です。物が豊かではなかった昔、人々は質素と倹約を常に行い、子どもの教育の上でもそれを大切な行いとしてきました。地位が高く、**経済的に豊かな人**であればなおさら、「謙虚」であることをよしとしたために、質素倹約に努めました。

　「節約」は、「節度」ある生活をするための一つの具体的な行動でもあったのです。

point (*fushime*) in his life.

Economize

In economic terms, *setsudo* ("restraint") can be seen in the concept of *setsuyaku* ("to economize").

In simple terms, *setsuyaku* is the beauty of not wasting things, of living an **austere** life as one develops the concrete knowledge of how to economize.

The Japanese phrase *mottainai* ("**What a waste!**") was at one time popular at the United Nations. At the time, the phrase was used in reference to taking care of natural resources, being sure to make full use of things. For example, as one uses a bar of soap in the bath, the soap gradually wears down to a small piece. Rather than throwing that piece out, one should put that piece aside in a net bag. By doing this over time, the bag will eventually become full of small pieces of soap, and then one can wash oneself without the need to buy additional soap or a new sponge. Throwing away small pieces of soap would be described as *mottainai*, while saving the small pieces would be called *setsuyaku*.

Shisso ("**simplicity**") and *ken'yaku* ("**frugality**") are two essential elements of *setsuyaku*. In the old days, when people did not have much, they lived simply and frugally and passed these values on to their children. Given the importance of being *kenkyo* ("modest") for **well-off persons** or those of high rank, it was all the more the case that they also lived simply and frugally.

Setsuyaku is one concrete way of living a life in tune with the value of *setsudo* ("restraint").

節制

　「節度」という価値観において、「節約」がそれを支える経済的な行動であるならば、「節制」は人の心や体を健全に保つための方法論です。

　日本には、「腹八分」という言葉がありますが、これは**満腹を戒め**、「節制」しようという言葉です。

　「過ぎたるは及ばざるがごとし」という言葉は、何事も過度に行えば、充分でないときと同じように害があると戒めることわざで、「節制」とは、常に自分の限界を意識しながら、生活をマネージしていこうという考え方を示します。すなわち、「節度」ある生活態度が「節制」なのです。

　「足るを知る」という言葉があります。これも、自分が、どのような状態で満足できるのかということを知って、それ以上を求めず自らの「節<ruby>節<rt>ふし</rt></ruby>」の中で謙虚に生きようということを意味します。「節制」とは、まさにこうした考え方に支えられた人の生き方への指針といえましょう。

　「節制」した毎日を送る中で、人は社会の中で争うことなく、「和」を保ち、同時に自らの精神性も高めてゆくことを理想とします。

　この考え方は、封建時代の道徳教育の中枢にあり、仏教哲学の中にもそれをみることができるのです。

　自分という風船の空気を抜き、欲望を抑え、自我やエゴをコントロールすることを学ぶことが「禅」などで語られているのです。「節制」は、そうした哲学を毎日の生活に投影させた、生活への戒めに他なりません。

Moderation

If *setsuyaku* is the means by which material things are economized, then *sessei* is the means by which aspects of the human mind and body are similarly used without waste.

In Japanese, there is a phrase: *hara hachi bu* ("80% of the stomach"). This means to avoid **indulgence** and instead eat with *sessei* ("moderation").

Another Japanese saying admonishes us that "**having too much is the same as not having enough.**" In other words, *sessei* means that one must always understand one's limits and live within them; *sessei* means living a life with an attitude of *setsudo* ("restraint").

There is a similar phrase in Japanese: "**know what is sufficient**." This also means knowing what is enough to satisfy oneself and not asking for more than that, living modestly within the circumstances of that particular period (*fushi*) of one's life. It may be said that *sessei* is indeed a compass for leading a life supported by this way of thinking.

The ideal in a life of *sessei* is to maintain one's *wa* ("harmony"), not creating friction with others, while at the same time strengthening oneself spiritually.

This way of thinking was evident in the ethical teachings of the feudal period and could also be seen in Buddhist philosophy.

Zen teaches the need to escape from the insular bubble that is oneself, controlling selfish desires and the ego. *Sessei* must be seen as the imperative to include such thinking in our everyday lives.

6

情

Feelings

情

「情」とは人の思いや感情を表す漢字です。

人の喜びや悲しみ、楽しみや苦しみを生み出す心のエネルギーを、日本人は「情」という言葉で言い表すのです。

よく、欧米の人が、日本の映画やテレビドラマは、感情表現の場がしつこく**ウエットすぎる**と批判します。その一つの理由として、日本人はジェスチャーや言葉を使って、感情を強く表現しないため、どうしても感情表現の場が長くなってしまうことが挙げられます。

恋人同士の別れの場を表現するときに、「愛しているよ。またすぐ逢いたい」と言えばすむ場面を、**じっと涙をこらえて、**目頭がすこし潤んできたときに、恋人を乗せた列車が出発するというように、むしろ言葉を交えずに表現したほうが、日本人の心に響いてくるのです。

特に、言葉はできるだけ少ない方が、説得力があるとするコミュニケーションスタイルをもつ日本人にとっては、言葉に表さない「情」を**知覚する**ことが、相手を理解する大切な要因となるのです。

このコミュニケーションスタイルが、日本人特有の「情」への価値観を**育みました**。すなわち、「情」は言葉に表さない人間の気持ちへの美学によって支えられた価値観なのです。

日本人は、「情」を感じるとき、相手に対して何かしてあげなければというモチベーションを抱きます。そうしたモチベーションへの期待が、日本人特有の人間関係における**紐帯**を育むわけです。そしてビジネスであろうが個人であろうが、「情」を感じ合うとき、お互いに打ち解け合って話ができるのです。日本人特有の身近な人への甘

Feelings

Jō is the Chinese character for "feelings."

The Japanese express the energy created by such emotions as happiness, sadness, pleasure, and distress in the word *jō*.

Westerners often criticize Japanese movies or television dramas for being **too emotional**. One reason that can be given for this is that the Japanese tend to express their emotions indirectly rather than by using a lot of words or gestures; this means that it takes longer for such emotional scenes to be played out.

When two lovers part at a train station, for example, rather than simply saying, "I love you; I want to see you again soon," it is more emotional for the Japanese to play out the scene without words, **with tears slowly building in the eyes** and then trickling down the cheeks as the train leaves.

Particularly for the Japanese, whose communication style uses as few words as possible, it is critical when trying to understand another person to **grasp** the *jō* that is being expressed nonverbally.

It is this communication style that **brought about** the Japanese value of *jō*. In other words, it is the beauty of nonverbal human emotions that brings true life to this value.

When the Japanese feel *jō*, that is when they are most motivated to act. It is in turn this motivation to act, generated by *jō*, which creates the **bonds** of *ningen kankei* ("human relationships"), which are so important to the Japanese. It is here, too, that one can see the concept of *amae* ("**dependency**") in relationships with those to whom one is close.

えの構造がそこに見えてくるのです。

｜人情

　「情」という価値観をもっと端的に示しているのが「人情」という価値観です。**洋の東西を問わず**、人は誰でも親しい人に対して愛情を抱いています。また、めぐまれない人に接すれば、たいていの人には同情心がうまれます。この、他の人に対する個人的な感情を「人情」といいます。

　たとえば、刑事裁判で、被告人が**不幸な境遇にあったために罪を犯した**であろうと思われる場合、判事が**軽い判決を下す**ことがあります。この場合、判事は「人情」によって心を動かされたとされ、人々はその判決に拍手するというわけです。

　こうした話はよく時代劇の題材になります。「人情」によってビジネスや公の決済が影響を受けることは、日本ではむしろよいこととされているのです。状況によっては、「情」を加えることはむしろプラスなのです。

　実は、日本人は、「ビジネスはビジネス」として、個人の「情」とビジネスを切り離すべきものだという考えになかなか馴染めません。本来は客観的に意見を交換し、判断を行うべきビジネスでのやりとりが、日本では「ハートとハート」のやりとりとして受け取られ、それがもとで人間関係が上手くいかなくなったり、取引が不調におわることもあるのです。

　もちろん、日本でもビジネスと個人の情とを混同しては

Personal Feelings

Ninjō is the value of *jō* ("feelings") expressed in a more direct manner. It is the willingness to embrace the love of all people **without question as to their nationality**. It also means that there is a sympathy for those whom one comes into contact with who have not been so fortunate in their lives. These emotions that one has for others are called *ninjō*

For example, if a court is trying a criminal, the judge may **give a lighter sentence** if the person in question committed the crime **due to the unfortunate circumstances of his environment**. In that case, it would be said that the judge had been moved by *ninjō* and people would applaud his decision.

This type of story is often seen in *jidai geki* ("samurai tales"). In other words, when *ninjō* moves a person to be generous in making a business or public service decision, this is considered a good thing in Japan; and depending on the situation, the more generous the better.

It is true that it is difficult for most Japanese to accept the idea that "business is business" and separate their personal feelings from business. Although business should be conducted in a manner in which ideas are objectively exchanged and judgments made on that basis, in Japan it is instead common to conduct business on a "heart-to-heart basis," and this can often lead to broken relationships and bad business deals.

Of course in Japan, the **principle** of not mixing business

いけないという**道徳律**は存在します。それだけに、人は反対意見を述べたりするときは、「人情」を意識し、気を使い、相手の**立場をたて**ながら表明するのです。

　その表明のしかた自体が、欧米の人からみると、ビジネスと個人の「情」とが混在しているようにみえることもあるようです。

義理

　「義理」とは、人と人とが人間関係を**維持して**ゆくための義務や務めを意味する言葉です。

　たとえば、ある人に大変**お世話に**なった場合、その人に対して「義理」があると人はいいます。そこで生まれる義理を意識して、受けた**恩恵に報いる**ことが道徳的に求められているわけです。

　日本の場合、この人と人との縛りが伝統的に強かったといえましょう。特に、江戸時代に代表される封建時代には、身分や性別、そして年齢など、さまざまな立場での役割が厳しく設定されていました。そして、役割**を逸脱する**ことや、自らの立場を超えて行動することは禁じられていたのです。

　したがって、「義理」に縛られながら、その縛りを超えた人と人の「情」との間にはさまれて葛藤するテーマが、歌舞伎や文楽などの**伝統芸能**でよく取り上げられました。たとえば、親の「義理」に縛られて婚約させられた娘と、その娘に恋する若者の物語などが、それにあたります。「義理」と「人情」というテーマです。

義理と人情をテーマにした古典で一番よく語られるのが、江戸時代に活躍した近松門左衛門の心中をテーマに扱った人形浄瑠璃や歌舞伎の「世話物」と呼ばれるストーリー。

with one's personal feelings also exists. When one is faced with someone taking an opposing position, however, one takes *ninjō* into account and is careful to do what one can to **accommodate** that person.

It is this very tendency of Japanese to take *ninjō* into account in such cases that apparently leads Westerners to believe that Japanese are mixing business and their personal feelings.

Obligation, Duty

Giri means the responsibility and effort that go into **maintaining** a relationship between one person and another.

For example, if one is **indebted** to another for a favor done, then it is said that one has *giri* to the other person. In that case, Japanese ethics require that one be well aware of the *giri* incurred and **repay the favor**.

In Japan this type of connection from person to person has traditionally been strong. Especially during the feudal Edo Era, one's position was strictly fixed according to one's rank, sex, age, and so on. It was not possible to **deviate from** one's rank or make an attempt to better oneself within society.

Because of this, conflicts between one's obligations (*giri*) and one's feelings (*ninjō*) were a common theme in the **traditional performing arts** such as the *kabuki* or *bunraku* ("puppet theatre"). An example of such a conflict would be a daughter who became engaged to one man to fulfill her *giri* to her father, while her true affections (*ninjō*) were for another young man.

　ごく日常的な「義理」といえば、夏や年の暮れに、仕事上あるいはふだんの付き合いでお世話になった人に贈り物をしたり、挨拶にいったりする習慣があります。今でこそ少なくなりましたが、上司が引っ越しをするときに、部下がそれを手伝うといった習慣も挙げられます。

　多くの場合、「義理」はこうした上下関係での道徳律と深く関わっています。上司にお酒に誘われて、恋人とのデートの約束をどうしようかと迷うのも、現代版の「義理」と「人情」といえましょう。

　最近は、こうした場合、若い人は「人情」を**優先する**と、年輩の人はぼやいているのもまた事実なのです。

恩

　「義理」という考え方に最も影響を与えるのが「恩」という価値観です。

　封建時代には、君主は自らの部下である侍に**俸禄**を与え、その侍の身分を保障します。その地位は、その侍一代ではなく、代々受け継がれることが普通でした。

　この身分と生活の保障を君主から受けることが、侍にとっての「恩」です。侍はその受けている「恩」に報いるために、時には**命をかけて**君主に仕えなければなりません。すなわちそれが侍の「義理」というわけです。

　現在でも、「**あの人には恩がある**」と人はよくいいます。

ルース・ベネディクトの『菊と刀』は、「恩」という概念を、アメリカ人が理解できるよう詳しく解説したことで知られる。

This would be a classic *giri-ninjō* theme.

In terms of everyday life, an example of *giri* would be giving gifts and making the rounds of greetings during the summer and at the end of the year to those whom one is indebted to for social or business favors. Another example, which is rare nowadays, would be for subordinates in a company to help their boss move.

As in these cases, *giri* often has a strong connection to the ethics of relationships between those in higher and lower positions. It might be said that a modern version of a *giri-ninjō* conflict would be for a boss to invite one out for a drink on a night when one already had a date set with one's girlfriend.

It is a fact that older people today are not happy with the way that younger people tend to **put** *ninjō* **ahead** of *giri*.

Social Debt

The social value known as *on* has heavily influenced the concept of *giri* ("obligation").

In the feudal period, a lord would pay his samurai a **stipend** and guarantee their position in society. It was the usual practice to guarantee that rank not just to that particular samurai, but to his descendants as well.

Having received a position and the guarantee of a living, the samurai would have incurred *on*, and in order to repay that social debt, the samurai would loyally serve his lord, at times having to **put his life on the line**. In other words, this was the samurai's *giri* ("obligation").

Even today, people often speak of "**having** *on*" to a

自分を育ててくれた親への「恩」、知識を与えてくれた教師への「恩」、そしてスキルを教えてくれた上司への「恩」などがそれにあたります。

人は「恩」に対して、それに報いるように努力することが求められます。「恩」と「義理」との関係は、一時的なものではなく、多くの場合一生その人の人間関係に影響を与えます。昔は「恩」を忘れることは、最も**非道徳的な**こととして、非難されていたのです。

日本人の心の中に深く残る「恩」という発想は、日本人がビジネスの上でも単にビジネスライクに物事を進めるのではなく、個人的な感情で判断をする原因の一つにもなっています。たとえば、「恩」のある人の子どもだからということで、昇進や就職に手を加えることも時にはあり、それがさまざまな**不正**の原因となることもあるのです。

逆に、あの人には「恩」があるからということで、その人が死んだ後も、その子どもや遺族の相談にのろうとする行為は、美徳であるともいえるでしょう。

「恩」という発想には、こうした功罪両面があるようです。

なさけ

「情」という漢字にはもう一つの読み方があります。それが「なさけ」です。

「情」を通わせるとき、特に上の立場の者が下の立場の者に対して**手心を加える**ことを「なさけをかける」といいます。

また、「なさけ」とは人に対して特別に考慮して、その

particular person. Common examples would be the *on* that is incurred by a child to his parent, or a student to his teacher, or an employee to his boss.

It is expected that those who incur *on* will make efforts to repay it. In most cases, *on* and *giri* are lifelong obligations, not something which affects one only for the short-term. In the old days, forgetting to repay one's *on* was considered a very **unethical** act and would be heavily criticized.

The concept of *on*, which is so deeply rooted in the character of the Japanese, is one reason why they are not able to take a more "business-like" approach to business, instead allowing personal feelings to affect their judgments. For example, **inequities** often result from giving favorable consideration for hiring or promotion to the child of someone to whom one has incurred *on*.

On the other hand, it is a thing of beauty to see someone reach out to assist the child or other family members of someone to whom one has incurred *on* after that person has died.

In this way, the concept of *on* would appear to have both merits and demerits.

Compassion

The Chinese character used to write *jō* ("feelings") can also be read as *nasake*.

When the character is read as *nasake*, it in particular **denotes the compassion** that a person in a higher position shows towards a person in a lower position.

Nasake describes the feelings a person had when he took

人が助けられ、あるいは利益を得たりするように配慮する心を指す言葉です。すなわち、「なさけをかける」という行為は、上の立場の者が、人に対して恩を与える行為に共通しているのです。封建時代には、女性の立場は低いものでした。たとえば、女性がお金持ちの男性や、身分の高い侍の情婦になると、その女性は相手から「なさけ」を受けたと表現します。もちろん、その場合、女性はその男性に生活の面倒をみてもらうことが期待されているわけです。

また、身分の低い者が何か**間違い**を犯して、自らが責任をとるときに、上の立場の人が特別の配慮でその罪を軽減したりすることを、「**なさけをもって**」と表現します。

秩序の掟によって社会が成り立っている中で、「なさけ」は唯一例外をもって人を救済する情の概念に支えられた抜け道であったともいえましょう。その「なさけ」という概念は、現代社会においても、「先輩」、「後輩」、「同期」などの人間関係の中で活用されることはしばしばです。たとえ仕事の結果はよくなくても、「**あいつは頑張ったから**」という理由で、先輩の上司が後輩の部下の失敗を許すケースなどは日常よくある光景なのです。

内と外

人と人との複雑なしがらみの中で、その人の「情」と「義理」との関係がわかり、心を許して話ができる信頼関係が構築されたとき、その人は自分の人間関係の「内」に

special considerations to see that someone was helped or benefitted in some way. In other words, this act of a person in a higher position "employing *nasake*" in effect results in the person in the lower position being given *on* ("a social debt"). In the feudal period, women were in a low position in society. For example, if a woman were to become the mistress of a rich man or a samurai of high rank, it would be said that this woman had received *nasake*. Of course, in such, a case it would be expected that the man would cover the woman's living expenses.

In another example, if a person in a low position were to take responsibility for some sort of **offense** he had committed, it would be said that "***nasake* had been employed**" if a person of higher rank gave special consideration and lesssened the penalty for the offense.

In a society based on strict order, *nasake* may have been the only means of allowing one to save people through compassion. There are many cases today of the concept of *nasake* being used in the relationships between *senpai, kōhai, and dōki*. For example, it often happens that even if the results are not good, a boss who is also a *senpai* will forgive his subordinate, saying that "**he made his best effort.**"

Inside and Outside, Social Circle

When one is able to navigate the *shigarami* ("barriers") of a relationship and understand the particulars of *jō* ("feelings") versus *giri* ("obligations") to the point that one can let one's

いると考えられます。

たとえば、家族や会社の親しい同僚は「内」の関係で、そこに入らない人は「外」の人と捉えられます。「外」の人とは、ある程度お互いがよく知り合うまで、率直な付き合いを**控える**のです。

この「内」と「外」との境界線は、その人のおかれている立ち位置の違いによって変化します。たとえば、同じ村の人でも、家族からみると「外」の人ですが、違う村の人と比較すれば、「内」の人となります。外国の人を「外人」と呼びますが、この場合は日本を「内」と捉えているので、外国は「外」に他ならないのです。すなわち、「外人」とは「外の人」という意味なのです。

複雑な人間関係から発生する**齟齬（そご）や軋轢（あつれき）**といったリスクを軽減するために、日本人は伝統的に「内」と考える相手に対してのみ、本当の思いや情報を共有する傾向にあります。

「内」に迎えられるためには、何よりも、お互いを**公私ともに**よく知り合う必要があります。そして、「情」をもって話し合える関係になれば、「内」に入った仲間として情報が共有されるのです。

日本人がビジネスの関係においても、よく夕食を共にし、お酒を飲んで騒いだりする背景には、お互いに「内」の関係になろうとする意識が働いているのです。これは、外国人のように日本社会の「内」に入りにくい人にとっては、常にお客さんとして扱われ、親切にはされるものの、打ち解けることができないという問題に直面するリスクもあるのです。

日本を知る外国人は、「外人」という言葉に違和感を示す。いつまでも日本の社会に受け入れられず「外」の人として扱われることを象徴する言葉であると知っているからで、「Gaijin」としてそのまま皮肉をこめて使うこともある。

guard down and truly trust that person, then it is said that that person is *uchi* ("inside").

For example, a person who is not within one's family or close associates at one's company would be considered to be *soto* ("outside"), and one would **have some reserve** in dealing with that person until one got to know the person better.

How to distinguish between *uchi* and *soto* depends on the situation in question. For example, people in the same village who are not in the same family would be considered *soto* in terms of family, but those same people would be considered *uchi* in terms of the village versus people from outside the village. In Japanese, a foreigner is literally called *soto no hito* or *gaijin* ("outside person"). In this case, if we take Japan to be *uchi* ("inside"), then foreign countries must be seen as *soto* ("outside").

To reduce the risk of dealing with the **complications** of relationships, the Japanese have traditionally tended to only really open up to share information and personal feelings with people whom they felt were *uchi* ("inside") their social circle.

In order to be welcomed "inside" (*uchi*), it is necessary that two persons know each other well both **publicly and privately**. Then they will be in a position where they can open up to their feelings (*jō*) as persons "inside" the same social circle and freely share information.

In terms of business, it is common for Japanese to have dinner and drinks together as they attempt to build a relationship in which they can both be "inside." For foreigners, who may find it difficult to break into the social circle, there is the risk that they will continue to be treated politely as guests without being able to get their Japanese counterparts to open up to them.

　日本で「内」に迎えられるためには、まずビジネスライクな付き合いをやめて、プライベートな話を共有し、一緒に過ごす時間を増やしてゆく努力が必要なのかもしれません。

┃ 本音と建前

　「内」と「外」との関係を最も象徴的に表した言葉が、「本音」と「建前」です。「本音」とは、「内」の同じグループのメンバー同士で語られる本当に思っている内容のことで、「建前」は、**表向きの、**あるいは外交的なメッセージや言葉を指す表現となります。

　日本人ならではのコミュニケーションスタイルを理解している人同士であれば、「本音」と「建前」とを見分けることは比較的簡単かもしれません。しかし、外国から来た人は、「建前」を聞いて、それを「本音」と勘違いし、あとになって思うように事が進まずにびっくりすることもしょっちゅうあります。残念なことに、この「本音」と「建前」を理解していない人から見れば、あたかも日本人が嘘をついているように誤解することもあるかもしれません。

　日本人から「本音」のメッセージを受け取るには、「内」に入ること、あるいは相手の属する「内」に加わる人を通して間接的に情報をとることが求められます。そして、何よりも、そうした人を介して相手を夕食などに招待し、お酒を酌み交わしながら、打ち解けてゆくことも大切です。

　「本音」と「建前」は、外国の人にとって、**最もやっかいな**日本人のコミュニケーションスタイルのひとつなのです。

In order to be welcomed "inside" in Japan, it is necessary to not have a purely "business-like" relationship and instead to be sure to increase the time spent in sharing private interests.

True Feelings and Facade

Two words that most closely represent the relationship of *uchi* ("inside") and *soto* ("outside") are *honne* and *tatemae*. *Honne* refers to the true feelings that are spoken by those who are "inside" (*uchi*) the same group, while *tatemae* is what is spoken **for show** or to be diplomatic.

For those who understand the Japanese communication style, it is relatively easy to see the difference between what is *honne* and what is *tatemae*. However, it is quite common for non-Japanese people to hear what is *tatemae* and misunderstand it as *honne*, later being surprised when things don't progress as they had thought they would. Unfortunately for those who cannot tell the difference between *honne* and *tatemae*, misunderstandings may sometimes arise where it is felt that the Japanese are not telling the truth.

In order to get the true intent (*honne*) of a Japanese person, one will be expected to become a member of his "inside" (*uchi*) group or go through someone who is inside the group. Above all else, it is then important to take that person out to dinner and have a few drinks with him in order to get him to fully open up.

For the foreigner, understanding *honne* and *tatemae* may be one of the **most challenging** aspects of the Japanese communication style.

円満

　「円満」とは、お互いに「情」を大切にし、「和」が保たれることによって、**人間関係がうまくいっている**ことを示す言葉です。

　家庭円満といえば、親子関係などがうまく機能し、家族全員が**仲良く暮らしている**状態を指しています。

　円とは、丸いことを示す言葉です。日本人は、どこかが**突出する**ことのないまるい状態が究極の「和」の状態であると考えるのです。

　「**全てが丸く収まった**」という言葉がありますが、これは問題を解決し、関係者全てが納得した状態ができたことを意味する表現です。ロジックではなく、情によってこそ、お互いに**妥協**し、「円満」な関係が構築できると日本人は考えます。そうした意味では、もし欧米の人が自らの主張をあまりにも強く押し付けてきた場合、それは「円満」を阻害するものとして日本人に不快感を与えることがあるかもしれません。

　「**出る杭は打たれる**」という格言があります。飛び出している杭が打ち込まれるように、**突出した**考えやあまりにも独創的な行動は拒絶され、葬り去られるというのがこの格言の意味するところです。

　ある意味でこの格言は、和を保つには適したアプローチですが、反面では、リーダーシップをとりたがらず、集団での意見調整にエネルギーを費やすという結果をもたらすことにもなるのです。

Harmonious

Enman refers to a situation in which feelings are mutually treated with respect, and harmony is preserved, **leading to a good relationship**.

If one says that a family is *enman*, then we know that the relationships between the children and parents are good and that the whole family **gets along well**.

En means "circle." The Japanese think of a round shape with no parts **protruding** as a state of *wa* ("harmony").

The phrase *subete ga maruku osamatta* ("**it's all been peacefully settled**"), means that a solution to a problem has been found, and all of those concerned are satisfied. The Japanese feel that it is important to put feelings first, rather than logic, and **compromise** to build the "harmony (*enman*)" of a relationship. In this sense, if a Westerner insists too much on putting their own needs first, this may disrupt this harmony and make a Japanese feel uncomfortable.

There is also a phrase that "**the stake that protrudes will be hammered down.**" In other words, just as a stake that protrudes is hammered down, so will a **deviant** way of thinking or overly independent behavior not be accepted.

While this approach promotes harmony, it is also true that it can result in a reluctanace to take leadership as well as added effort required to reach a concensus within the group.

他人

「他人stranger」は見知らぬ人という意味で、この延長には「外国人foreigner」という言葉もある。誤ったイメージをあたえかねないので、公には"foreign national" "overseas national"を使うとよい。

「他人」とは見知らぬ人、あるいは自分とは特に関係のない人を意味する言葉です。それに対して深く知り合っている相手のことは「身内」と呼びます。

もっと端的にいうならば、「他人」とは自分が「情」をもって接する必要のない一般の人を意味します。「内と外」の概念での「外」に属する人をより明確に規定した言葉が「他人」なのです。

日本人は「他人」に対しては、本音を語ることはほとんどありません。

欧米では、「他人」でも道ですれ違うときは軽く挨拶をします。日本ではそうした光景はほとんどありません。さらに、あれだけ「和」を大切にし、お互いに気を使い、遠慮する日本人でありながら、朝夕の通勤列車などでは、「他人」をぐっと押して電車に乗ることに**躊躇しません**。

「他人」との人間的距離感は、欧米の人々にとっての「他人」と比べた場合、より遠いのではないでしょうか。

日本人は、声を掛け合うなど、お互いを意識すれば、その瞬間から和を保つためのモードにはいります。「他人」の度合いは、「内と外」の概念と同様、知り合えば知り合うほど薄くなります。挨拶をした瞬間から「他人」であっても気を遣い、相手の立場を考えつつ行動をはじめるのです。

日本人は、気遣いの必要のない、全く見知らぬ人、すなわち「本当の他人」のことを「赤の他人」と呼んで、全く自らの**視野**の外におくのです。

Outsider

A *tanin* is a person whom one does not know, or in other words, a person with whom one has no particular relationship. In contrast to this, a person with whom one is close is called a *miuchi*.

Putting it more directly, a *tanin* is a person with whom it is not necessary to engage one's feelings (*jō*). In the concept of *uchi* and *soto* ("inside" and "outside"), a *tanin* would fall into the "outside" category.

A Japanese rarely expresses his true feelings (honne*)* to a *tanin*.

Westerners easily greet people they don't know on the street, while it is unusual to see a Japanese do so. It is also true that the Japanese—who place such importance on treating others with respect and maintaining harmony—**will not hesitate to** push and shove strangers on the morning and evening rush hour trains, as these people are *tanin*.

Compared to Westerners, the Japanese feel a greater distance between themselves and *tanin*.

For the Japanese, once one person takes notice of another and words are exchanged, then the process of maintaining harmony begins. As with the concept of "inside and outside," the more one gets to know a person, the less one senses that person as a *tanin*. As soon as one person greets another, even if that person is a *tanin*, one must begin to take into account the concerns of the other person.

A person whom one does not know and about whom one need not have any concern is called *aka no tanin*; such a person is completely outside the **purview** of a Japanese.

7

忠

Loyalty

忠

　前章の「恩」の概念を思い出してください。

　人から「恩」を受けると、それに対する「義理」が発生します。

　「忠」は、その「義理」の中でも特に身分や立場の高い人に対して発生する義務を示す言葉です。

　「恩」を与えてくれた人に対して、しっかりと敬意を表し、行動をもってその人に対して尽くしてゆく考え方が「忠」です。したがって、「忠」という概念は、より身分の上下がはっきりしていた封建時代において特に強調された道徳的規範であり、そこから派生する行動規範となるのです。

　現代社会において、「忠」という意識をそのまま強要されることは少なくなりました。しかし、会社に対して忠誠心を持ち、時には自らを犠牲にしても会社のために労苦を惜しまず仕事をするという美学が、今でも日本社会には残っています。「忠」という意識は、日本人の心の奥深くに刻まれている遺伝子のようなものなのかもしれません。

上下

　「上」と「下」の概念は、「忠」と大変深く関わっています。

　今はもちろん存在しませんが、封建時代には、身分の「上下」が社会制度の基本でした。特に士農工商という4つの身分に人は分けられ、武士が最も高く、商人は最も低

Loyalty

Please recall our discussion of *on* ("debt" or "favor") in the last chapter.

One receives *on* from someone, and in turn one incurs *giri* (an "obligation").

Within the concept of *giri, chū* is the particular type of obligation that is **incurred** to someone of high rank or position.

The concept of *chū* means respecting and serving a person from whom one has received *on*. In the feudal period, when rank and position were even more clearly defined, the **ethical norms** of *chū* were therefore all the more emphasized.

In today's modern society, the awareness **per se** of *chū* is not as strong as it once was. However, even today in Japan, people will have loyalty to their company and from time to time sacrifice themselves by taking on undesirable assignments for the greater good of the company. It may be that this sense of *chū* ("loyalty") is grafted deeply into the DNA of the Japanese.

Hierarchy

The concept of "higher" rank and "lower" rank strongly influences *chū* ("loyalty").

During the feudal period, there was a strict system of hierarchy, although such a class system does not of course exist today. At that time, society was split into four classes: samurai, farmer,

忠

い地位にありました。そしてたとえば武士の中でも、幾層にも身分が分かれていたのです。

この身分の「上下」という考え方は、現代社会では、たとえば上司と部下、先生と生徒の間でみられます。あるいは生け花や茶道の学習にみられる家元制度などに強く受け継がれています。産業によっては、**官と民間**の間にも、大企業とその**下請け**の間にも、上下の意識が歴然と残っています。

「上下」の概念が、日本では長い間差別の原因となってきたことも事実。アメリカは「上下」の意識がない反面、移民同士の対立に起因する人種差別が長い間続いた。これを乗り越えるためにアメリカにできた法律を、公民権法「Civil Rights Act」という。

日本では、相手の人格が自らより「上」の立場にあるか、「下」にあるかによって、言葉遣いも変われば、応対も違ってきます。もちろん、欧米でも立場の「上下」はあり、相手がどういう立場かによって、ある程度は応対を変える習慣はあります。しかし、人と人とは**基本的に**平等で、挨拶の方法にそれほどの変化があるわけではありません。

しかし、日本では「上下」関係の「義理」に縛られた行動様式が、欧米よりも際立っていることは否めないようです。

もちろん、法律的にも制度の上でも、「上下」による差別は日本でも違法行為です。しかし、「上下」に関する人の意識は法的な規制とは別に、日本社会の根本原理として維持されているのです。

目上、目下

「上下」の考え方は、単にビジネスなどの社会生活の中

craftsman, and merchant, with the samurai at the top and the merchant at the bottom. Within the samurai class, there were several additional distinctions of rank.

In Japan today, *jōge* can still be seen in the relationship between boss and subordinate, or between teacher and student. It is also still very much alive in the disciplines of flower arrangement and the tea ceremony, for example. Depending on the industry, there may be *jōge* relationships in place between **government agencies and private companies**; and clearly a *jōge* relationship can be seen between large companies and their **subcontractors**.

In Japan, one's language and the way one interacts with another person will differ depending on whether the other person is "higher" or "lower" than oneself. For Westerners as well, the concept of "hierarchy" exists and the way one person greets another will differ to some degree depending on the status of the other person. **In principle**, however, people are treated as equals, and there is not as large a difference.

In Japan, however, it cannot be denied that the concept of *jōge* plays a greater role than it does in the West, due to the way in which *giri* ("obligation") strongly affects actions.

Of course, in Japan as well today, discrimination based on *jōge* is against the law. That said, the concept of *jōge* is still deeply rooted in Japanese society.

Higher and Lower Position

The concept of *jōge* ("hierarchy") is still clearly present in Japan

のみならず、個人の生活環境の中にも歴然と残っています。

　その代表的な概念が、自分より年上の者に敬意を表する「目上」、「目下」の概念です。もちろん、「目上」が年上で、「目下」が年下です。社会的な地位での「上下」が関わらない限りにおいて、「目下」の人は常に「目上」の人ときっちりと区別されます。「目下」の人が「目上」の人へ敬意を払い、丁寧に接することによって、「目上」の人にかわいがられるといった「情」の交換がそこにあるのです。

　「目上」と「目下」の価値観が社会生活で最も顕著にでるのが学校や会社での「先輩」と「後輩」という概念です。

　「先輩」とは、先に学校に入学したり、会社に就職した人のことを意味し、あとから入ってきた若い人を「後輩」といいます。「先輩」は「後輩」を指導し、「後輩」は「先輩」に敬意を払いながら、学校や会社で活動するノウハウを学ぶのです。

　最近は少なくなりましたが、日本では**年功序列**という考え方があり、何年会社に勤めたかによって、評価や雇用条件が決められます。

　人は、社会の中で、まず相手が「目上」であるかどうかを察知し、さらに学校や会社では「先輩」であるかどうかを見極めながら行動します。

　そして最終的に、上司と部下という「上下」関係と、「目上」と「目下」、「先輩」と「後輩」という概念を組み合わせながら、お互いに気遣ってコミュニケーションをしてゆくのです。

　こうした背景からか、日本人は見知らぬ相手に年齢をき

today, not only in the broader society, but in private relationships as well.

A representative example of the concept of *me-ue* and *me-shita* is the respect one pays to someone who is older than oneself. In this case, the older person is of course the *me-ue* party, and the younger person is the *me-shita* party. If there are no other hierarchical considerations, it will be expected that the *me-shita* party will be properly differential to the *me-ue* party. While the *me-shita* party will pay the proper respect to the *me-ue* party, the *me-ue* party will in turn feel an obligation to take care of the *me-shita* party.

The concept of *me-ue* and *me-shita* can be seen most clearly in the related concept of *senpai* and *kōhai*. A *senpai* is a person who started school or joined a company or some other organization before one, while the junior party in such a relationship—the person who joined the organization later—is the *kōhai*. Knowledge is passed on within schools, companies, and the broader society as a *senpai* instructs the *kōhai*, and the *kōhai* in turn pays the proper respect to the *senpai*.

Although it has become less common recently, a so-called **seniority system** exists in Japan in which companies base promotions and compensation on the number of years a person has been employed.

In social settings, people will first confirm if the person they are dealing with is *me-ue*; they will then confirm whether the person is a *senpai* from their school or company or other organization.

In the end, people will seek the proper means of communication by taking into account all of these factors: *jō* or *ge*, *me-ue* or *me-shita*, *senpai* or *kōhai*.

Because of the importance of age in establishing whether

くことがよくあるのです。これは欧米にはない、欧米の人には理解しがたい慣習といえるのかもしれません。

同期

　「先輩」、「後輩」という概念と密接に関係するのが「同期」という考え方です。「同期」とは、同じ年に入社したり、入学した仲間を指す言葉です。

　日本の場合、たとえば大学を卒業する年齢は浪人や留年をしなかったとして22歳です。したがって、多くの人が同じ年齢で就職し、会社に入ります。そうした人々が同期となるのです。

　大学などでも同期の人々は、卒業後もお互いに連絡を取り合いネットワークします。あたかも欧米で有名ビジネススクールの卒業生のネットワークがあるように、彼らも横の繋がりをもって活動し、時には強い連携によってお互いに協力し、情報交換を進めるのです。

　また、ビジネスで、ある会社にものを売り込む場合、その会社に学校時代での同期の人間がいれば、より商談が進みやすくなります。もちろん、そこに先輩や後輩が転職していたりした場合も同様です。

　現代社会はよりダイナミックに変化しているために、以前ほどではなくなりましたが、伝統的な日本社会は、「先輩」「後輩」の概念と、「同期」の概念とによって縦糸と横

someone is *me-ue*, Japanese will often ask a person's age, even if they don't know the person well. Since this custom does not exist in the West, it may be difficult for Westerners to understand why the Japanese do this.

Classmate

The concept of *dōki* is closely related to *senpai* and *kōhai*. A *dōki* is someone who starts school or joins a company in the same year as oneself.

Those who attend university in Japan, for example, graduate when they are 22, assuming that they haven't taken extra time to pass the entrance exam or repeat a year. Many people then start working in a company at the same age, and those who start in the same year become *dōki*.

Dōki from the same university will continue to stay in touch through their own network after graduation. In the same way that Westerners who graduate from famous business schools will maintain a contact network, *dōki* from Japanese universities will also keep up their contacts, using these strong connections to promote cooperation and the exchange of information.

When arranging a sale, negotiations will be easier if a *dōki* from one's university is at the company to which one is selling. Of course the same is true if there is a *senpai* or *kōhai* at the company as well.

Because today's society is more dynamic, such ties are not as strong as they once were, but still in order to understand Japan today, one must grasp the concepts of *senpai, kōhai, and dōki,* all

糸が織られ、できあがっているわけです。

奉公

　封建時代に「恩」を受けた人に期待される行動が「奉公」でした。

　この「恩」と「奉公」との関係は、単にビジネスライクなものではありません。侍は、その一生、さらにその祖先から子孫へと、君主や上司から「恩」を受け、それに対する「義理」として「奉公」するわけですから、その**紐帯**は深く、単なる人間関係を超えた「情」と「義理」とで結ばれたものでした。

　滅私奉公という言葉があります。その意味するところは、私情に左右されず、「恩」を受けた人に対してとことん仕えるという倫理観を示しています。時には、自らの命を捧げて君主を守り、その行為に対して君主は、その人物の家族や子孫へもさらなる**利益を与え**てゆくのです。こうしてこの滅私奉公という、ある意味自己犠牲の考え方は**正当化**されるのです。

　滅私奉公をすることによって、人は「恩」を与える者に対する「情」の深さを示し、その「情」によって気持ちを動かされた上に立つ者は、さらに「奉公」する者に**愛情を注**ぐのです。

　このプロセスの残滓が、現代社会にもあります。個人の予定よりも会社や上司のニーズを優先して残業をする意識など、一見過去の価値観と思われがちな「奉公」という意識が、現在の日本人にも受け継がれ、大切な価値観となっていることには驚かされます。

of which helped to weave the fabric of traditional Japan.

Service

During the feudal period, it was expected that *on* ("social debt") would be repaid through *hōkō* ("service").

This relationship of *on* and *hōkō* was not simply a business arrangement. For a samurai, the *on* that was incurred extended throughout his own life and stretched back to his grandfather and forward to his grandchildren, resulting in a deep **bond** with his lord that was based on *jō* ("feelings") and *giri* ("obligation").

Messhi hōkō ("**self-sacrificing service**"), is an expression that means to not be swayed by personal feelings in repaying through service the *on* that one has incurred. On occasion a samurai would have to give up his life in order to protect his lord, and in turn the lord would **grant** additional **benefits** to that samurai's family and descendants; in this way there would be **compensation** for the sacrifice (*messhi hōkō*) of the samurai.

Through one's service, a person shows the depth of his feelings (*jō*) towards the person to whom he has incurred *on* ("social debt"), and in turn that person will be further moved and **show his affection** for the person providing the service.

The product of this process continues to be found in Japan today. To a surprising degree, the values of *hōkō,* which had been thought to be old and passé, have continued on—in the way a Japanese will work overtime to put the needs of his boss or the company before his personal ambitions, for example.

忠義

　武士の社会では「奉公」という概念を、特に「忠義」とい
う考え方に結びつけていました。「忠義」は、武士が自らの
主君に対して命をかけて「奉公」することを示す言葉です。
　「忠義」は「武士道」の根本を貫くストイックな精神で、
主君を守るために死の恐怖をも克服して**忠誠を保つ**こと
を侍に要求している価値観です。
　したがって、武士は徹底的に「忠義」を尽すことが美徳
とされ、そのために常に精神的な修養と、武道の稽古、**学
問の研鑽**が求められていたのです。

　「奉公」の概念が、武士に限らずより一般的に、「恩」に
報いるための行為を示しているのに対し、「忠義」は武士
が「奉公」するための意識を表す言葉として、彼らの**倫理
的な核**となった言葉です。
　忠臣蔵という日本人なら誰でも知っている物語があり
ます。この物語は、ある君主が恨みのある身分の高い人物
に刀で切りかかり、傷つけたことからはじまります。君主
がその人物に貶められていたという事実にも関わらず、徳
川幕府は君主に切腹を申しつけます。その君主のために、
配下の武士たちが浪人となり討ち入りを果たし、君主の敵
をとったという実話なのです。その後、配下の武士たちは
全員切腹を命じられます。

　しかし、彼らは死の恐怖を乗り越えて、**亡き主君のため**
に働いたわけで、そうした彼らの行為は、まさに「忠義」
を全うしたとして、人々に語り伝えられたのです。

Loyalty

In the society of the samurai, the concept of *hōkō* ("service") was closely related to the concept of *chūgi* ("loyalty"). In other words, *chūgi* meant putting one's life on the line in service for one's lord.

Chūgi is at the root of everything to do with the samurai spirit; it is a basic value which requires the samurai to overcome the fear of death in order to **maintain his loyalty** to his lord.

It was expected that the samurai would do everything possible to maintain this virtue of loyalty, and that in order to do this he would constantly undertake spiritual, military, and **scholarly training**.

The term *hōkō* ("service") was used in a general way to refer to the service undertaken to repay *on* ("social debt"); in the case of the samurai, *chūgi* was at the **ethical core of** their *hōkō*.

There is a tale in Japan called *Chūshingura* with which all Japanese are familiar. Based on a true story, the tale begins with a certain lord pulling a sword at court and wounding a high official who had been maltreating him. Despite the fact that the lord had been responding to the bullying of the official, he is ordered to commit *seppuku* ("suicide") by Tokugawa shogunate. His **retainers**, who have become *rōnin* ("masterless samurai"), then carefully plan and execute the assassination of the official. For this, the *rōnin* themselves are ordered to commit *seppuku*.

This action on the part of the *rōnin*, overcoming their fear of certain death in order to revenge their **deceased lord**, has been passed down over the years as an example of what is precisely meant by *chūgi*.

忠

「忠義」は、日本人があこがれる**精神的な美学**であるともいえましょう。

孝

「目上」、「目下」という年齢差に起因する人間関係の中で、最も大切なものは親子の関係でした。

封建時代、武士は親子の間でも厳しい「上下」の隔たりがあり、父親は常に一家の長として、家族を監督する立場にあったのです。

そして、子どもは「目上」である両親に対して敬意を表し、常に大切に遇してゆくことが、**儒教道徳**の上からも強く求められていました。当時、武士の子どもは、両親に対してあたかも身分の異なる人に接するように、言葉遣いも変えていました。

この親に対する心構えを「孝」または「孝行」といいます。

「**孝行**」の発想は、日本のみならず他の多くの国にも見られ、とくに儒教道徳の影響の強い韓国で受け継がれています。

現在、親子の関係は以前とは比べものにならないほど、カジュアルになりました。「孝」に基づいた行動様式は、今ではほとんどみられません。

しかし、「孝行」という概念はよい**価値観**として、今なお教育の現場などでも取り上げられているのです。

Loyalty is a **spiritual virtue** highly prized by the Japanese.

Filial Piety

Of all *me-ue* ("higher") and *me-shita* ("lower") relationships, the most important one is that between parent and child.

During the feudal period, there was a strict *jōge* ("hierarchy") maintained between parent and child, with the father at the top overseeing the entire family.

Under these **Confucian morals**, children were expected to respect their parents and always give them due consideration. At the time, children would speak to their parents as if they were persons of different rank.

This type of attitude towards one's parents was called *kō* or *kōkō* ("filial piety").

Filial piety is a concept that exists not just in Japan but in many other countries as well, including Korea, where the influence of Confucian morals is strong.

Compared to the past, the relationship today between parent and child has become much more casual. It is rare now to see actions being taken based on the principles of *kō*.

However, at schools and other places of learning, filial piety is still often used as an example of a strong **social value** that should continue to be respected.

忠

しがらみ

　「目上」、「目下」、「先輩」、「後輩」、「同期」、そして親子
など、日本社会を彩るさまざまな縦の構造は、ある意味とて
も複雑で、それに対応するコミュニケーションスタイル
も多岐にわたります。そんな複雑な人間関係を日本人は
「しがらみ」と呼ぶのです。

　「しがらみ」とは、元々水の流れを止める設備のことを
意味します。これが、複雑な人間関係を表現する言葉とな
ったのは、人間関係が生んださまざまな「義理」に縛られ
て人間の自由な行動が束縛されるからに他なりません。

　したがって「しがらみ」という概念は、そのまま「義理」
にも繋がり、そして社会でのさまざまなモラルとも直結し
ます。

　「義理」と「人情」の狭間で苦しむ人とは、まさにこの社
会の「しがらみ」に捉えられて苦しむ人のことを意味して
いるわけです。

　日本人が、自らの人間関係のことを「しがらみ」と表現
する背景には、長い歴史の中で培われたさまざまな常識や
硬直した社会制度に、日本人そのものがとらわれているこ
とを示していることになります。

　しかし、同時に、「しがらみ」は、人が自らの勝手で行
動するのではなく、相手の立場や気持ちを考えてどのよう
に動くかを判断させる、大切な価値観でもあるのです。

Barriers

Japan's **vertical society**, with its highly varied types of relationships such as *me-ue, me-shita, senpai, kōhai, dōki,* and so on is quite complicated, and requires one to constantly make choices as to communication style. The Japanese call these types of **complicated relationships** *shigarami.*

The word *shigarami* originally refers to a device used to stop the flow of water. The word took on its broader meaning in the sense that a person's freedom to act was restricted by the *giri* ("obligations") that he would incur.

In this way, the concept of *shigarami* is connected to the concept of *giri* and to other ethical and moral considerations in society.

It would certainly be the case that a person dealing with the difficult conflict between *giri* ("obligation") and *ninjō* ("personal feelings") would be an example of a person caught in the *shigarami* of society.

The use of the word *shigarami* to **refer to** the difficulty of relationships reflects the common practices of this **inflexible** society, which have developed over a long period of time.

However, at the same time it must be said that *shigarami* is a positive social value since it prevents people from acting **for selfish reasons** and instead encourages them to carefully consider the position of others.

8

神

The Gods

神

　日本人にとっての「神」とは、多くの場合、日本古来の宗教である**神道**でのさまざまな「神」を意味します。

　神道は、明治時代に天皇を中心とした近代国家を建設しようとしたときに、国教化され、天皇の**権威**を象徴する宗教として政治的に利用されたために、大きな誤解を与えてきた宗教でもありました。

　神道は、**元来**ヒンズー教と同じ**多神教**で、日本各地に育まれてきた多彩な宗教でした。神道の信奉者は、滝や岩、そして湖や大木など自然の中に神が宿ると考えていました。日本人は農耕生活を営むにあたって、その地域を象徴する木や岩の精霊に**豊作を願い**ました。そして村々の安全を願うための宗教行為の集大成でもあったのです。

　実際、石や自然物を**崇め**たり、水で**清め**たりする宗教行為は、北から南までアジア全般でみることができます。日本人にとって、そうした自然を象徴する事物の神秘を崇め、その前で身や心を清めることが、大切な**宗教上の行為**だったのです。神道は、こうした目的のために山にこもって修行し、鍛錬する山岳信仰などをも育みます。

　キリスト教や仏教などと違い、**偶像**を信仰の対象とせず、常に自然と向かい合うことが神道の特徴で、唯一例外として「神」の象徴として自然を映し出す「鏡」などが崇拝されることがあるのです。

　この古代から伝わる神道の考え方が、後年に大陸から伝

キリスト教社会では自らの神を他と区別して、Godと大文字のGを使って表現する。他に、世界で信仰されるさまざまな神を、godとは別に、deityと表現することもある。

The Gods

When Japanese refer to *kami*, they usually mean the gods of the **Shintō religion**, which has been in Japan since ancient times.

Due to the fact that Shintō was instituted as a state religion for political purposes at the time of the Meiji Reformation, using the **prestige** of the emperor as its symbolic head, this religion has sometimes been misunderstood.

At its roots, Shintō was a diffuse system of beliefs that developed over time in local areas throughout Japan and, like Hinduism, had **multiple gods**. The followers of Shintō believed that the power of these gods resided in waterfalls, rocks, lakes, large trees, and other objects of nature. As an agricultural society, the Japanese would **pray for an abundant harvest** to the spirits symbolized by these objects; these religious rites also became an opportunity to gather together to pray for the safety of these various villages.

From the north to the south throughout Asia, it is possible to find religions that **worship** rocks and other objects in nature and that perform **purifying** rites with water. For the Japanese, who worshipped the mystery symbolized by nature, purifying one's body and soul before these objects was an important **religious rite**. With this objective in mind, various types of ascetic training in the mountains developed.

Unlike Christianity or Buddhism, there is no worship of **idols** in Shintō, where the worshipper is always at one with nature; the only exception to this would be mirrors used to reflect the symbols of nature.

The native Shintō later mixed with elements of Buddhism

来した仏教と重なり、日本人独特の**精神的価値観**が育まれます。仏教の修行の中に、神道的な身を清める発想が加わり、実際仏教の寺院に仏を崇める堂の横に、神道での「神」を祭る神社が置かれたりするのも、日本の宗教の特徴といえましょう。

　キリスト教とは違い、日本人にとっての「神」とは、人が自らの罪や贖罪を意識して対峙する「神」ではなく、自らを取り巻く自然への敬意と、清らかな自然に向かい、自らをも清めてゆく考えの中で創造されたパワーなのです。

禊
みそぎ

　岩や大木など自然の造物に魂や神が宿るとする神道において、最も大切とされる行為がそうした精霊に向かうにあたって、**身を清める**行為です。

　この身を清める行為のことを「禊」といいます。特に、神道などで、神のそばに仕える者は、水などで身を清め、常に清潔にしておくことが求められました。

　この「禊」の行為が、その後さまざまな形で日本の伝統の中に残るようになります。たとえば、お祭りで体に水をかけたり、元旦に冷たい海に入って一年の**無病息災を祈ったり**といった行為が日本各地にみられます。さらに、今でも山岳信仰で、滝にあたって身を清める風習があることなど、例をあげればきりがありません。

　日本人は風呂が好きで、シャワーではなく、湯船につかる習慣があります。湯船につかった後で、改めて体を洗う

from the Asian continent to create the unique **spiritual values** of the Japanese. This mixing of Shintō and Buddhist elements is a trait of religion in Japan, and can be seen in such things as Shintō-like purifying in Buddhist training; it is also not uncommon to find a Shintō shrine right next to a Buddhist hall of worship.

Unlike Christianity, where people are expected to **atone** to a god for their sins, the appeal of Shintō for the Japanese is to be found in the respect paid to nature and, through being unified with the purity of nature, to in turn become pure oneself.

Purification

The act of **purifying oneself** before rocks, trees, and other objects of nature where spirits and gods reside is considered to be very important.

Such an act of purification is called *misogi*. For those in particular who participate in the rites of Shintō, it is expected that they will purify themselves with water, always keeping themselves clean.

The act of *misogi* can be found in many different forms in the traditions of Japan. For example, throughout the country one can see people pouring water over themselves at various festivals; or one might see people jumping into cold ocean water on New Year's Day as they **pray for good health in the coming year**; or one might find people standing under a waterfall as part of spiritual training in the mountains. There are countless examples.

The Japanese preference for taking a bath instead of a shower—washing themselves outside the tub before getting

風習は、こうした「禊」のしきたりにその原点があるのかもしれません。

「禊」の行為は、単に体をきれいにして神に向かうだけではなく、行為を通して心の穢れも清らかにしてゆくものと信じられています。

昔の日本人にとって、日々の生活の中に**区切りをつけ**て、心と体を清め、改めて神に向かう行為は、生きてゆく上での大切な「けじめ」でもありました。

今も、神社にお参りをする前は、神社の入り口や前にある水場で手を洗い、口をゆすぎます。その後で、日本人は神に向かって商売や家庭の平安を祈願するのです。

穢れ
けが

「禊」と深く関わる概念が「穢れ」です。

「穢れ」とは、心身ともに穢れた状態を示します。神の前に立つとき、人は穢れのない状態でなければならず、そのために「禊」を行うのです。

純潔という言葉があります。これは世界の多くの国にある古典的な価値観であり、文化現象ですが、処女であること、また子どものように純粋であることへの美学が神道における「穢れ」という発想の対極にもあるのです。

実際、神道では子どもには大人にない神的なパワーがあると信じられており、婚姻するまでの女性が純潔であることは、封建時代の道徳律などとあいまって、昔は大切なことであったのです。

女性の純潔を尊ぶ風習は、神道のみならず世界の多くの宗教にみられる。代表的なのはキリスト教での聖母マリア、さらには仏教での釈迦の誕生にまつわる伝説などがある。

in—may be related to this custom of *misogi*.

The act of *misogi* is not simply a matter of cleaning one's body; the Japanese also believe that this is a cleansing of the soul.

For the Japanese of old, it was important to **mark the distinction** between everyday life and the time one would spend before the gods by first properly purifying the body and soul.

Even now, before entering a shrine to pray, one will wash one's hand and rinse out one's mouth. It is only after purifying himself that a Japanese will then pray to the gods for the welfare of his family or business.

Defilement

A concept that is closely related to *misogi* ("purification") is *kegare* ("defilement").

Kegare refers to both the defilement of the body and the soul. One must be purified before standing in front of the gods in order to not present a defiled self.

Many countries have the traditional value of "**purity**" in their cultures. In Shintō, this concept of being pure in the way that a virgin girl or child is pure also exists.

In Shintō, it is believed that children have spiritual powers that adults do not, and traditionally, it was considered ethically important that a woman remain pure until her marriage.

　子どものように純真ではなく、処女のように純潔ではない状態が穢れた状態とされ、人々は大人になってからも、神社などでそうした「穢れ」を**払おう**としたのです。

　「穢れ」とは、単に見た目が汚いということを超えて、**邪悪な心**を持つことそのものを指す言葉として捉えられていたのです。

清楚

　「禊」の概念からもわかるように「**清める**」行為は、神道ではとても大切な宗教行為です。

　純粋で美しい自然のパワーを前に、さまざまな穢れを払い、単純で清らかな状態でそれに接することが、神道での大切な価値観であるといえましょう。

　「清楚」とは、自らやその周囲を整え、**無駄なものを持たず**、清らかな状態でいることです。

　よく日本人はきれい好きだといわれます。たとえば、レストランでテーブルをきれいにしたり、旅館で**布団をたたんでおく**など、さまざまな事例が挙げられます。

　身の回りをきれいに保つことは、多くの日本人の心に長年にわたって**染み渡った**風習であるといえましょう。

　こうした風習の原点に、神道で身を清め、自然と向き合い、質素に生活する美意識があるのではないでしょうか。

　また、さらにその奥には、「徳」の章で触れる「潔い」心構え、すなわち言葉で飾ることなく、静かに物事に接することへの美学も隠れています。

　もちろん、物質文明が席巻する現代社会において、日本

For adults, who were no longer pure like children or virgins, they would try to **rid** themselves **of** their *kegare* at shrines or other places of worship.

Kegare was not simply a matter of being physically unclean; in looks; it also referred to the **wickedness** in a person's soul.

Neatness

As we saw in the concept of *misogi*, the act of **purification** is a very important religious rite in Shintō.

Ridding oneself of defilement and appearing before the purity and beauty of nature in a simple and pure state oneself are important basic values of Shintō.

Seiso means to maintain a pure state by putting oneself and one's **surroundings** in order, **with no waste**.

It is often said that the Japanese like cleanliness. For example, at a restaurant, people will clean up their own table; at an inn, people will **put away their own** *futon*.

Over the course of many centuries, this habit of keeping the area about oneself clean has been **instilled** in most Japanese.

It would appear that an awareness of beauty has grown out of these customs of purifying oneself and being at one with nature.

As we will see in Chapter 12 when we discuss *toku* ("virtue"), the concept of *isagiyoi* ("pure" in the sense of not being boastful or wasteful in words) is also related to this broader sense of purity in Shintō.

Of course in today's materialistic society, it is certainly a

人がこの美意識通りに生きているかといえば疑問も残ります。また、以前に比べ、日本人もかなり自己表現が豊かになり、**饒舌**にもなりました。

しかし、日本人が憧れる理想の中に、こうした道徳律があることは事実といえるでしょう。現代社会の現実と、こうした日本古来の理想へのあこがれとの**矛盾**に今まさに日本人は直面しているわけです。

清廉

「清楚」という価値観を、**さらに深めた**言葉が「清廉」という概念です。

「清廉」という言葉の意味することは、**私心**がなく、清らかな心もちのことです。実際、古来中国や日本では、儒教道徳の中で、私心を捨てて公の為に生きることの美徳が語られています。

中国に、「**清廉潔白**」という熟語があり、それは私心がなく、どこからみても恥じることのない公正さを示す言葉として日本でも使われています。

日本に**儒教的な考え方**が伝わったのはかなり昔のことですが、とくに封建時代には、「恩」と「奉公」の概念が強く根付いていたため、「清廉」な人格を育むことの重要性が、特に強調されました。

この儒教道徳に、神道の「清楚」という価値観が加わったことで、日本流の「清廉」が生まれたのでしょう。

question as to what extent the Japanese are still able to live their lives with this awareness of the beauty of nature. Also, compared to the past, the Japanese have become more **talkative** and better able to express themselves.

That said, it is true that the Japanese still cherish these older values of purity of spirit and paucity of words. The Japanese today are confronted by this **contradiction** between the reality of the current society and the ideals of the past.

Integrity

The concept of *seiren* ("integrity") takes the concept of *seiso* ("neatness") **one step further**.

Seiren means to have a pure heart, with no **personal ambitions**. In the ancient Confucian philosophy of China and Japan, personal interests were put aside for the greater good of the public.

In Chinese there is a phrase *seiren keppaku* ("**integrity and purity**"), which is also used in Japan and means to put aside personal interests and act absolutely impartially, avoiding all dishonor or shame.

Confucian thought entered Japan early on, but it was particularly during the feudal period that the concepts of *on* ("social debt") and *hōkō* ("service") drove the importance of becoming a person of *seiren* ("integrity").

It is probable that the addition of the Shintō concept of *seiso* ("neatness") to Confucian ethics resulted in the Japanese version of *seiren*.

日本では、中国を介して**伝わってきた宗教**や価値観は、仏教にしても儒教にしても、試行錯誤のなかで、神道と対立するものではなく、**共存する**ものとして受け入れられました。そして、日本独自の価値観と、外から持ち込まれた価値観が混ざり合う中で、日本人独特のものの考え方が育まれてきたのです。

「清廉」や「清楚」という考え方は、たとえば仏教での「禅」、そして侍の価値観でもある「武士道」などと混ざり合い、シンプルな中に美しさを求める発想を培ったのです。芸術の世界でみるならば、こうした発想の**究極の表現**が、**石庭**などにみられるミニマリズムであるといっても過言ではないでしょう。

シンプルな中に美を求める考え方は、日本人の生き方という価値観から、芸術的な表現方法にまで、幅広く影響を与えていったのです。（日本人の美の概念については第13章を参照）

願

日本人は一般的に神社で神に自分の実利的な願いが叶うようにお祈りをします。

たとえば、子どもが試験に合格して、高校や大学に進学できるように祈る人もいます。**商売が繁盛**するようにとか、個々人によってさまざまな祈願をするのです。

こうしたお願いを、真剣に行うことを「願をかける」といいます。「願」とは、「禊」を行って自らを清め、時には自分の欲望を抑えて心から穢れをはらい、神に対してお願いをする行為です。

Religious beliefs and values such as Buddhism and Confucianism, which **were brought to** Japan from China, came to **co-exist** with Shintō through a process of trial and error, rather than conflicting with it. Through the mixing of these native and imported ways of thought, the unique value system of the Japanese was developed.

For example, the concepts of *seiren* and *seiso* mixed with the Buddhist values of Zen and the samurai values of *bushidō* to develop a way of thinking which prized simplicity and beauty. In the world of art, the **ultimate expression** of this may be in the minimalism of the Japanese **rock garden**.

Finding beauty in simplicity has influenced a wide range of Japanese thought from the values of the way one lives to the way one expresses oneself in art. The Japanese concept of beauty will be discussed in more detail in Chapter 13.

Request

It is common for the Japanese to pray to the gods at shrines for their wishes to **come true**.

For example, one might pray for a child to pass a test or get into a good high school or university; or one might pray for the **prosperity of one's business**. People pray for a variety of things.

When one wishes to make a particularly important request, the Japanese use the phrase *gan wo kakeru*. When making such a request, one will first purify oneself, ridding oneself of defilement and controlling one's desires, before praying to the gods.

　たとえば、お酒の好きな人は、「願」をかけている間は、お酒をやめるという行為で自分のお酒への欲求を抑えたりするのが一般です。

　神道を**強く信奉**し、山を歩き、滝にあたって自らを清める行為を通して、修行を続ける人が昔から日本にはいました。彼らは仏教の影響も受け、**経を読み**ながら、「禊」を行い、心身を鍛えて**悟り**をひらけるようにと「願」をかけます。

　そうした人たちからみた場合、「願」とは単なる利益を得るために「神」に祈るという行為を超えた、精神的な高みを求めるための真剣な行為で、その行為を通してこそ望みがかなえられるという考え方なのです。

　そして、「願」をかけて神に祈る行為を日本人は「祈願する」といいます。祈願とは「祈り、そして願う」という意味の熟語です。

大和魂

　第二次世界大戦中、日本人を**鼓舞する**ために盛んに語られた言葉が、この「大和魂」という言葉です。

　大和とは、古代の日本を示す言葉で、戦争中には**軍国主義**に利用され、この「大和魂」を強要された多くの若者が、戦いで命を落としてゆきました。

　元々、「大和魂」とは、神道に根ざした清らかさを根本に、自然と共にそこに宿る神々を大切にし、生活を整えてゆく精神を指す言葉でした。

For example, if a person is fond of alcohol, it is common for him to give it up while the request.

Since ancient times, **fervent** Japanese **believers** in Shintō purified themselves and strengthened their bodies and minds through walks in the mountains and standing under waterfalls and other training. Over time, these believers were also influenced by Buddhism, and in the Buddhist tradition, would **read sutras** and pray for **enlightenment**.

Gan is more than simply making requests of the gods; it is an attempt to improve one's spiritual being, and through that process, perhaps one's requests will be answered.

The Japanese also use the word *kigan* (literally, "pray request") when praying to the gods to answer requests.

Japanese Spirit

During the Second World War, the phrase *yamato damashii* ("Japanese spirit") was often used to **inspire** the Japanese people.

Yamato is the ancient name of Japan. During the war, this phrase was abused by the **militarists**, and many young men were sent to their deaths in the name of *yamato damashii*.

Originally, *yamato damashii* was deeply rooted in Shintō, and referred to the spirit a person developed in purifying himself while being at one with the gods who resided in nature.

　明治時代になり、神道が皇室の宗教として国家によって統率され、**国粋主義**と融合したとき、「大和魂」は日本人の強く優れた精神性を表現する言葉となり、以降この言葉は**国家威信**を強調するために使われるようになったのです。そして最終的には、「大和魂」に「忠義」や「滅私奉公」の価値観が集約され、日本が**全体主義国家**として戦争へと傾斜していったのも事実です。

　確かに、神道は**日本独自**の宗教です。しかし、その**ルーツ**をたどれば、アジア各地に残る**自然信仰**や、ヨーロッパの森林信仰などにも結びつく、世界的に共有できる宗教でもあったわけです。「大和魂」はそんな神道を大切にする日本人の精神を表す言葉だったのです。

In the Meiji Era, Shintō became a state religion with the emperor at its head, and combined with **nationalism**, *yamato damashii* came to mean the strong national spirit of the Japanese. Thereafter the phrase was used to enhance **national pride**. And then later, in the 1930's, *yamato damashii* was combined with the concepts of *chūgi* ("loyalty") and *messhi hōkō* ("self sacrificing service"), as the nation slid down the slippery slope to a **totalitarian state** and war.

Shintō is in fact a religion **unique to Japan**. However, if one **traces the roots** of Shintō, one can find much in common with other **animistic religions** in the rest of Asia, that as well as in Europe. *Yamato damashii* is a phrase that expresses the importance Japanese place on the spirit of Shintō.

9

仏

Buddhism

仏

　日本に仏教が伝わってきたのは7世紀の頃ではないか
といわれています。以後、仏教は時には権力者と**結びつき**
ました。後になると、権力者と結び権威となった仏教を批
判する僧が出てきて、新しい信仰が生まれました。以来、
仏教は民衆に広く伝搬してゆき、**多様な形で受け入れられ**
ていったのです。

　「仏」という概念も、初期の仏教のように仏陀その人と
深く結びついたイメージから、さまざまな流派が発展して
ゆく過程で、より人の**苦しみ**を救済する「神」のようなイ
メージに**置き換えられて**いきました。

　また、それと共に、禅のように修行を通じて自らの中に
「仏」を見いだすという**内省的なもの**から、ひたすら**念仏
を唱え**、そのことによって**来世での救済**を期待するという
ものまで、信仰の方法も多様に変化してきたのです。

　さらに、日本古来の神道とも融合して、共に信仰の対象
となったのも日本の仏教の特徴といえそうです。
　神道には、**来世**に対するイメージが弱く、自然界に宿る
さまざまな神を信仰し、そこからのご利益はむしろ**現世**に
対するものでした。そんな日本人に来世観を与えたのが
仏教なのです。
　もともとインドに生まれ、中国を通して日本に伝わって
きた仏教ですが、現在私たちが日本で目にする仏教のほと
んどが、日本人独自の宗教観によって変化してきた、日本
ならではの仏教となっている点は、興味深いことであると
いえそうです。

Buddhism

It is said that Buddhism came to Japan in the seventh century. At some point, Buddhism became **tied to** the power structure in Japan. Later there was criticism of that association from certain elements of the priesthood, and as a result of that, other sects came into being. Thereafter, over time, Buddhism was spread widely among the people, **taking many forms**.

While in its early period, Buddhism was more directly associated with the Buddha himself; in later times, as more sects developed, Buddhism was **repositioned** more closely in association with the "gods" as a belief to save people from their **suffering**.

Together with this development, Buddhism moved from being primarily a **meditative discipline**, such as Zen, in which one sought enlightenment, to a more diverse belief system, which also included many sects more centered on **chanting** as a way of finding **salvation in the next world**.

Buddhism also combined with the native religion of Japan, Shintō, to create Japan's unique form of Buddhism.

In Shintō, there is not a strong connection to an **afterlife**; rather, the belief is in the elements of nature and how those elements can benefit one **in this life**. It was Buddhism that encouraged a Japanese belief in the afterlife.

It is interesting to note that although Buddhism originated in India and came to Japan from China, the Buddhism we see in Japan today is primarily a product of the unique religious beliefs of the Japanese.

自力と他力

　禅のように、自らが行う修行を通して**信仰を深めてゆこ**うという考え方を「自力」といいます。

　それに対して、ただひたすら**念仏を唱える**ことによって、来世での救済が約束されているというのが「他力」という考え方です。

　「他力」の発想は、より多くの人を救済しようとする**大乗仏教**の流れによるものといわれています。

　特に平安時代には**阿弥陀信仰**が広まり、貧困や病苦、そして戦乱に苦しむ民衆へと受け入れられてゆきました。念仏を唱えれば、阿弥陀仏によって死後、極楽に迎えられるという考え方で、この信仰を**抱く**人々の輪は、16世紀には大衆運動へと発展し、**為政者**をも脅かしてきたのです。

　一方、禅宗のように「自力」を重んじる考え方は、武士などの支配階級に拡大してゆきます。

　このようにして、「自力」と「他力」という二つの発想は、日本の風土の中で、「自力」の禅と「他力」の浄土宗、あるいは浄土真宗として育っていったのです。

　現在でも「自力」、そして「他力」という言葉はよく用いられます。「人に頼らず、仕事は自力で開拓しなければ」といったように、宗教**とは離れた**次元でこうした言葉が使用されているのです。

Self-power and Other-power

Seeking through self-discipline, as in Zen, to **deepen one's beliefs** is known as *jiriki* ("self-power").

In contrast to this, seeking one's salvation in the afterlife through **chanting to the Amida Buddha** is known as *tariki* ("other-power").

It is said that *tariki* came from the grass roots movement of **Mahayana Buddhism** to save more people.

Particularly during the Heian Period in Japan, the **creed of Amida** spread, as the common poor and sick and those affected by war found its message of salvation through chanting appealing. In the 16th century, the number of people **embracing** these beliefs grew to the point that they became a threat to the **ruling class**.

On the other hand, sects like Zen, with its emphasis on *jiriki,* became popular with the samurai ruling class.

In this way, the primary sects of Buddhism in Japan developed: the Zen of *jiriki* and the Jōdoshū and Jōdoshinshū of *tariki*.

Even now, the words *jiriki* and *tariki* are often used in conversation. For example: "Rather than asking someone else, one must do the work on one's own (*jiriki*)." In phrases like this, we can see how these words are used **apart from** their religious origins.

あの世

　仏教での死後の世界、すなわち来世のことを、人々は**俗語**で「あの世」といいます。「因果」の項でも解説しますが（第10章）、人はこの世での行いをよくすれば、「あの世」では**極楽**にゆくことができ、またよき人として生まれ変わるとされています。

　仏教が時代とともに日本で変化し、哲学としての仏教から信仰としての仏教へと変化する中で、この「あの世」の発想が大きく強調されてきました。それが、前項で紹介した「他力」の考え方と関係しながら、浄土宗、浄土真宗、そして日蓮宗といった新しい宗教運動へと発展し、現代に至っているのです。

　「あの世」があるということは、人々が現世で苦しんだり失敗したりする上での**保証**であり、救いであるといえましょう。そして、「あの世」があるということは、人に魂があり、死後も霊魂となってその人が存在することを意味します。

　それが、日本での**葬儀**やその後の死者を弔うさまざまな儀式へと発展していったのです。

　日本でよく語られる**怪談話**の特徴は、そうした霊魂が現世に対する恨みや**執着**が強く、「あの世」に旅立てず、幽霊となって現れるというテーマです。

　たとえば、理不尽に殺された人が、殺人者の前に恨みをもって幽霊として現れるわけですが、その殺人者が処罰されたり、幽霊に悩まされて自殺したりした場合、幽霊となった霊魂は、安心して「あの世」に旅立ちます。

　そのことを俗語では「**成仏する**」というのです。すなわ

「成仏」は、「人は死ねば仏になる」というある意味で日本独特の発想。「悟る」ための修行とは関係なく、皆「成仏」できるという「他力」の発想がそこにみえている。

The Other World

The world after death in Buddhism, or in other words, the afterlife, is called *ano yo* ("the other world") **in colloquial speech**. In the section on *inga* ("cause and effect") in Chapter 10, we will discuss how people who conduct themselves well in this world will go to **paradise** in "the other world" and then be reborn in favorable circumstances.

As Buddhism changed with the times in Japan and developed from a philosophy into a religion, this concept of "the other world" was emphasized more. As noted in the last section, this development was related to the concept of *tariki* and led to the founding of the Jōdoshū, Jōdoshinshū, and then later the Nichiren sects.

It may be said that the existence of "the other world" acts almost as an **insurance policy** for salvation for those who suffer or fail in this world. In "the other world," a person continues to exist as a spirit after his death in this world.

That spirit is honored in Japan in **funerals** and other ceremonies held after a person's death.

There are many **ghost stories** in Japan about spirits who continue to be bitter and **obsessed** with this world and are not able to go on to "the other world."

For example, a person who was murdered may go on to "the other world" only after the murderer has been executed or been haunted into committing suicide.

Going to "the other world" is called *jōbutsu* ("**becoming a**

ち、**恨み**や**執着**を捨てて、やっと「仏」の境地になって「あの世」、すなわち極楽に旅立ったというわけです。

もの の 哀れ

　仏教は、人の死を見つめる宗教でもあります。したがって、そこには**はかない人生**へのセンチメンタリズムが含まれています。

　元来、仏教は、人や宇宙の移り行く姿を捉え、自らの欲望を抑えて自然な姿に心を戻してゆく**自省的な**宗教であり、哲学でした。

　それが日本に伝来し、中世の矛盾の多い現世にあって、人々が来世に救いを求めるセンチメンタリズムへと変化してゆきました。

　たとえば、桜は春ほんの数日間花を咲かせ、あっという間に**散ってしまい**ます。この**移ろい**の中に美学を見いだしたのが、「ものの哀れ」という美意識です。

　人も、いつ死を迎えるか予想できません。特に昔は、子どもでも大人でも、あっけなく「あの世」に旅立ちます。それは桜と同じように哀れなもので、人のはかない人生に「ものの哀れ」という美学を見出したのです。

　平安時代以降、「ものの哀れ」という発想は文芸作品などに多くみられるようになりました。それが仏教での「他力」の発想と**影響を与え合い**、より宗教的な情緒へと変わ

Buddha") in common speech. In other words, when a person is finally able to rid himself of the **bitterness** and **obsessions** of this world, then he is able to go to "the other world" of the Buddha, which is paradise.

Pathos

In facing death and dealing with the **fleetingness of life**, an element of sentimentalism has developed in Japanese Buddhism.

In its origins, Buddhism was a religion and philosophy that dealt with the changing circumstances of humans and the universe, as people sought to return to their natural selves through **self-reflection** and the control of desires.

However, when Buddhism came to Japan and was faced with the conflicting realities of the middle ages, it evolved to meet the needs of those looking for salvation in the next world, and became more sentimental as it did so.

Cherry blossoms are one example. They bloom for only a few days in early spring before **being blown off** the trees. The sad beauty seen in this **transition** is what is meant by *mono no aware*.

No one knows when he will die. Particularly in the olden days, it was common to die suddenly at any age. As with the sad beauty of the brief life of the cherry blossoms, so it is with the *mono no aware* of the brief life of humans.

Starting in the Heian Period, one can see many examples of *mono no aware* in works of literature and art. The Buddhist concept of *tariki* ("other power") also **came to influence** *mono*

っていったのです。

　「ものの哀れ」は、日本人の美意識の奥にあって、現在でも多くの人が感じるセンチメンタリズムです。

　人ははかない存在であるがゆえに、お互いにその悲しみを癒し合うことは、「情」の価値観にも通じるものといえましょう。

無常

　「ものの哀れ」が美学的な発想であるとするならば、それを仏教の視点からみた概念が「無常」という考え方です。

　すべてのものは常に変化し、生まれた者は必ず死ぬ。そして栄華もいつか必ず衰退し、常に同じ状態を保つものはこの世にはないというのが、「無常」の考え方です。

　ある意味で、これは仏教において仏陀が最初に抱いた悲しみであり、「無常」を感じることから、仏陀が涅槃にいたる足跡がはじまります。

　日本では、そこに「ものの哀れ」で示したセンチメンタリズムが付加されていったのです。

　中世の叙事詩として有名な『平家物語』は、琵琶を奏でる法師によって全国に広められました。「諸行無常」という言葉が、その叙事詩の冒頭に語られています。これは「無常」という概念をより具体的に示した言葉で、この叙事詩では平家という12世紀後半に栄華を極めた一族が、ライバルの源氏に滅ぼされてゆく様子が語られています。「栄える者もかならず滅びる」と、叙事詩では語っているのです。

no aware, giving it a more religious feeling.

Mono no aware is a form of sentimentalism deeply imbued in the Japanese sense of beauty.

It is necessary for people to support each other in overcoming the sadness of this fleeting life, and in that one will also find the concept of *jō* ("feelings").

Transience

If one considers *mono no aware* ("pathos") to be an **aesthetic way of looking** at things, then the Buddhist equivalent would be *mujō*.

All things are constantly changing, and all living things will eventually die. All that is **glorious** will **decay**, and there is nothing that will be able to maintain its current form—that is the concept of *mujō*.

In a certain sense, this was the first sorrow that Buddha embraced, and it was from this point that he began his journey towards **Nirvana**.

The sentimentalism of *mono no aware* ("pathos") was added to *mujō* when in Japan.

In the Middle Ages, the epic **The Tale of the Heike** was spread throughout Japan by monks who sang while playing the *biwa* ("Japanese lute"). At the beginning of the tale, it is stated that "**everything is ephemeral, nothing is constant**." This is a concrete example of *mujō*, as the story tells of the decline of the once all-powerful Heike at the hands of their chief rivals, the Genji. "**The prosperous will always fall**" is one of the themes of the story.

　そして仏教の宗派の中には、「無常」であるが故に、阿弥陀仏を拝み、ひたすら念仏を唱えることで、苦しみのない来世へと迎えられると説く「他力」の宗派が生まれたのです。

悟り

　「諸行無常」を理解し、物事が起こり、変化する連鎖を見つめ、その連鎖の原因となる憎しみや欲望を絶つことによって、仏陀の境地へと至ることを「悟り」といいます。

　「他力」を唱える宗派では、ただひたすら念仏を唱えることで、阿弥陀仏が降りてきて人々を引き上げてくれると信じます。

　逆に、「自力」を唱える宗派では、さまざまな**修行**や**瞑想**を繰り返し、仏の心を体得しようと試みます。

　天台宗の本山である比叡山には、千日回峰行という**荒行**があります。**行者**は1000日にわたり比叡山や京都を毎日30キロから多いときは80キロ歩いて巡ります。そして700日目にある堂入りでは、堂の中で７日半飲まず食わず、眠らず、座らずの状態で**お経を読み**、毎晩谷底の**水を汲ん**で堂内の不動明王に供えるという行をこなさなければなりません。

Then, in order to deal with the transience and pain of this life, sects centered around *tariki* ("other power") developed, using earnest chanting to the Amida Buddha to bring peace and salvation in the next life.

Enlightenment

Having understood that "everything is ephemeral, nothing is constant," one then seeks enlightenment (*satori*). To do so, one rids oneself of one's enmities or desires by identifying their source and breaking the chain of such shortcomings, thereby advancing to the land of the Buddha.

Followers of the *tariki* sects believe that through earnest chanting they will be able to induce Buddha to come down and take them back to paradise.

On the other hand, the followers of the *jiriki* sects believe that through **self-discipline** and **meditation** they will be able to find salvation.

At the head temple of the Tendai sect, Hieizan, there is a **rigorous regimen of training** called *sennichi kaihōgyō* ("circling the mountains for one thousand days"). Over a thousand-day period, the **supplicant** walks between 30 and 80 kilometers a day around the Hieizan and Kyoto areas. Starting on the 700th day, there is a special period of seven-and-a-half-days during which the supplicant must **read the sutras** while not drinking, eating, sleeping, or sitting; each night he must also go down to the bottom of the valley to **fetch water** as an offering to the *Fudō Myōō*.

　こうして行を終えた人は大阿闍梨と呼ばれ、**京都御所**にも**土足**で参内できる特権を得ることができます。

　「悟り」を開くというのは、仏教徒にとっての共通の願いであこがれかもしれません。
　日本人の間にも、そのあこがれは静かに受け継がれ、今も多くの日本人の**心の支え**の一つとなっているようです。

禅

　日本の「禅」は、海外で最も広く受け入れられた仏教の宗派の一つといえましょう。
　鎌倉時代に中国から日本に伝わったとされる「禅」は、公案と呼ばれる師匠と弟子との**問答**を中心に修行をする臨済宗と、ひたすら座禅をする曹洞宗を中心に、全国に広がりました。

　座禅という瞑想を繰り返しながら、**自らを見つめ**、そこに「仏」に通じる仏性を見いだそうとする「禅」の行為は、「仏」と**対峙する**というよりも、瞑想を通して自らと向き合う宗教として、日本では特に**精神鍛錬**を日課とした武士階級に支持されてきました。
　「禅」は、日本文化にもさまざまな影響を与えてきました。
　質素で簡潔な生活習慣をよしとする「禅」の考え方に基づいて造られる禅寺にはじまり、そこでの作庭術や、茶道のたしなみ、さらには武術や武士の生活規範に至るまで、

Those who complete this rigorous training are called *daia-jari*, and as a reward, they are allowed to walk inside the **Kyoto Imperial Palace with their shoes on**.

For the followers of Buddhism, a desire to find *satori* ("enlightenment") is something they all have in common.

In Japan as well, the concept of *satori* has been quietly accepted and today is an important source of **solace** for many Japanese.

Zen

The Japanese sect of *Zen* is one of the most widely accepted forms of Buddhism in the West.

Imported from China during the Kamakura Era, *Zen* spread rapidly throughout Japan through the efforts of two sects: the Rinzai, which emphasized the **question-and-answer** approach between teacher and disciple known as *kōan;* and the Sōtō, which emphasized the meditative approach known as *zazen*.

Zazen's meditation places more weight on **self-discovery** than it does on **intercourse with** the Buddha, and in Japan this meditation became part of the daily routine of **self-discipline and spiritual training** for many in the samurai class.

Zen has also influenced Japanese culture in many different ways.

Starting with the temples themselves, which reflect *Zen's* emphasis on simplicity, the influence of *Zen* can be seen in such things as gardens, the tea ceremony, and the martial arts.

「禅」の影響をみることができます。

　ある意味で、今までみてきた日本人の価値観の中に、「禅」が見え隠れすることも否めません。たとえば、**雄弁であるより寡黙であることをよしとする価値観**や、自らの欲望を抑え、人に対応するコミュニケーションスタイルなども、「和」という日本人の基本的な価値観は、従来から日本にはあったにせよ、そこに「禅」の発想が加わることで、醸成されていったのではないでしょうか。

　禅宗が支配階級の道徳律の背骨として**浸透して**ゆくなかで、宗派の違いを乗り越えて、禅的な発想法を日本人が好んで、自らの生活規範の中に取り込んできたのです。

煩悩

　人間が持つさまざまな欲望のことを仏教では「煩悩」と呼びます。

　物欲、性欲、食欲、権勢欲など、煩悩には108種類あるといわれています。**除夜の鐘**という儀式が日本にあります。大晦日に寺院が108回鐘を鳴らして、この「煩悩」を清めようとするのです。

　仏教では、常にこうした「煩悩」をどのように**克服し**、「悟り」へと至るのかが課題となります。

　仏陀自身、長い間瞑想を続ける中で、自らを苛む煩悩と戦い、最終的にそれを克服して「悟り」の境地、すなわち**涅槃**に至ったといわれています。

　涅槃の状態を「寂静」と呼ぶように、それは「煩悩」によって心が騒ぐ状態を脱した、**何もない静かな状態**を指して

仏教での涅槃を意味するNirvanaはもともとサンスクリット語が英語になったもの。これは全ての煩悩を吹き消して悟りを開いた状態を示し、同時に釈迦の入滅（死）も意味する。

In a certain sense, it cannot be denied that *Zen* is present in some way in all of the Japanese values we have discussed to this point. For example, in the way that **silence is valued over talking**, or in the way that one's own desires should be controlled, or in the way that people communicate with each other—in all these ways we can see how the basic native value of *wa* ("harmony") was developed in tandem with *Zen*.

Zen **permeated** the ethical value system of the ruling classes, eventually transcending the sect to become an integral part of everyday life in Japan.

Worldly Desires

In Buddhism, the various desires that humans have are called *bonnō*.

It is said that there are 108 desires, including desire for wealth, sex, drink, power, and so on. In Japan there is a ceremony called *joya no kane* ("**New Year's Eve bell**") in which the temple bell is rung 108 times on the final night of the year in order to cleanse away the 108 desires.

In Buddhism, one must constantly **overcome** desire in one's attempt to reach enlightenment.

It is said that the Buddha himself meditated for a long period, battling with his own desires before finally overcoming them and finding enlightenment, or in other words, **reaching Nirvana**.

The state of Nirvana is called *jakujō*, and as its Chinese characters suggest, it means reaching a **state of nothingness**

います。

　日本では、静けさを静寂という言葉で現しますが、それもこの「寂静」からきている熟語です。

　日本人は「煩悩」という言葉をよく使い、「いやいや煩悩が多くてね」といえば、心配事や何かへの執着があって困っていることを示します。

　そんなとき、日本人はふとお寺巡りをしに京都に行ったり、人によっては四国八十八箇所というお寺巡りの巡礼をしたりしながら、自分を見つめ直そうと試みるのです。

空
くう

　空気の項で、「空」という漢字の意味するところはすでに説明していますが、ここでは、仏教における「空」とはなにかを見つめたいと思います。

　「空」とは、何もない状態、からっぽの状態を示します。「空」は、「虚空」という熟語によって、非常に小さな状態を示す言葉にもなります。それは、自我を限りなく小さくし、捨てることにより、自らの中に仏性を見いだそうとする仏教の根本的な考え方に通じる概念なのです。

　「虚空」というきわめて小さい単位から、さらに無限に近く縮小してゆくと、そこに涅槃寂静という最小の単位に到達します。これは東洋での実際の数字の単位であると同時に、仏教でいう静かに悟った状態をも示します。

　現代の物質文明では、生活を豊かにし、欲望を満たすこ

and quiet, having rid oneself of desires.

In Japanese, the word *seijaku,* which is an inversion of the characters for *jakujō,* is used to mean "tranquility" or "silence."

The Japanese often use the word *bonnō* in everyday conversation. They might say, for example, "I have so many desires (*bonnō*)." In this case, it means that they have worries or obsessions that are troubling them.

When faced with a situation like that, a Japanese will seek to right himself through self-reflection, perhaps worshipping at temples in Kyoto or making the rounds of the 88 temples in Shikoku.

Emptiness

In the section on *kūki* ("air"), we touched on the meaning of the Chinese character for *kū*. Here we will focus on the Buddhist implications of the character.

Kū **denotes** a state of nothingness, of being completely empty. In Japanese the word *kokū* also means a state of nothingness, but implies nothingness in a very small sense. One is able to find one's **Buddha nature** by shrinking down and ridding oneself of one's ego, the source of worldly desires.

Going beyond the already extremely small size of *kokū,* one continues to shrink one's ego **ad infinitum** until one reaches the **nothingness of Nirvana** (*nehanjakujō*). While this same word is used in East Asia as a **unit of mathematical measurement**, it also denotes the state of tranquility one reaches in enlightenment.

In today's materialistic society, people try to find spiritual

とが肯定され、精神の自由は豊かさによって獲得できるものとされています。ここに記す「空」は、それとは全く逆を示し、欲望を深めれば深めるほど、渇きは増してゆくと説いています。

　日本も**資本主義国**で、人々は金銭欲や物欲に体ごとつかっています。そして、確かに高度に発展した現代社会の中で、人々は精神的な疲れや渇きを抱いているのも事実でしょう。

　そんな日本において、人々は**心の奥底に**、こうした「空」への渇望、そして美意識を今なお抱いています。

　禅寺の簡素な庭を見るとき、どことなく**安らぎを覚える**日本人は数多くいるはずです。

無

　「無」と「空」とは非常に似た概念です。

　仏教では、**絶対的なものは存在せず、全てに原因と結果**があると説きます。したがって原因がなければ結果はなく、欲望がなければ、悩みは存在しなくなります。そうした**因果関係**を超えて、いっさい何も無い状態に自分をおくことが「悟り」である以上、「無」という考え方は、仏教の根本を示す概念といえそうです。この哲学的なものの見方は、実は日本人の行動様式にも**大きな影響**を与えてきました。

　「無」に至る最初の入り口は、**相対的、客観的**に物事をみることです。それは、自分からの発想のみではなく、相手が何を望んでいるかを知ることで、人と人との交わりから生まれる因果関係を理解することを意味します。

freedom through an affluent life and the satisfaction of their desires. *Kū,* on the other hand, is the complete opposite of this: the more one seeks to meet one's desires, the less fulfilled one will feel.

Japan is a **capitalist country**, and many people are able to meet most of their materialistic desires. It is also true that in this highly economically developed country, many people are spiritually exhausted.

Deep in their hearts, many of these same people would strongly like to experience the fulfillment and beauty of *kū*.

There are still many Japanese who can **feel** completely **at ease** when they experience the simplicity of a *Zen* garden.

Nothingness

Mu is very similar to the concept of *kū*.

In Buddhism, there are no **absolutes**, and all **effects** have **causes**. Because there is no effect if there is no cause, there are therefore no worries if there is no desire. Going beyond the **relation of cause and effect** to find enlightenment (*satori*) in nothingness (*mu*) is one of the basic concepts of Buddhism. This philosophy, this way of looking at things, has **had a large influence on** Japanese behavior.

The starting point for reaching *mu* is to look at things in a **comparative** and **objective** way. To do so, one must begin by taking the point of view of other people rather than one's own, and from there, one first understands the connection between cause and effect in human relations.

　この発想は、「和」の原理を持つ日本人には受け入れやすいものでした。自らの欲求を抑え、相手の意図を尊重しようという行動原理と、「無」へのアプローチが日本人のコミュニケーションスタイルに相乗効果を生み出すのです。

　これが、「遠慮」の価値観にも影響され、日本人**独特**の会話方法となりました。そして、これが自らのニーズをしっかりと伝えるべきとする欧米人との間の誤解を招くことも多いようです。

　「無」とは、どこにも中心がない状態です。

　すなわち、自分の欲求が中心ではなく、そこには必ず相手の望みという別の軸も存在しているわけです。

　究極の「無」とは、そうした欲求自体のない静かな状態に自らをおくことで、人へも救いを与える平安な状態が成立するという理想とつながるのです。

For the Japanese, who place such importance on *wa* ("harmony"), this is an easy concept to accept. In other words, the principle of controlling one's desires and respecting the intent of others meshes well with the concept of *mu* to achieve an effective communication style for the Japanese.

This is a conversation **characteristic** of the Japanese and reflects their sense of reserve (*enryo*). It seems that this reserved approach often leads to misunderstandings with Westerners, who tend to put their own needs first.

In the concept of *mu*, one has no center in oneself. In other words, the desires of others are always central, rather than one's own desires.

Taking oneself to the ultimate state of *mu* puts one in an ideal condition of tranquility, which in turn allows one to help others.

10

縁

Relationships

縁

ここでは、縁を Relationshipsとしたが、次頁の仏縁で訳されたように、「Fate 運命」という言葉に置き換えることもできる。縁には人間関係に起因するものと、運命による出会いや物事との巡り合わせを示す 2 つの意味があるためだ。

　「縁」とは、人と人との出会いや離別からできる人間関係、そしてそこで培われるつながりを指す言葉です。

　「縁」とは仏教で使われる言葉でもあり、仏によって結びつけられる人と人との関係を意味します。

　「袖触れ合うも他生の縁」という言葉が日本にはあり、それは、ちょっとした出会いでも大切にしなければという意味を含んでいます。相手に敬意を払い、相手と最大限の「和」を保ってゆくことが、「縁」が求める理想です。

　残念ながら、そうした考え方は、現代のビジネス文化の中では廃れつつあります。しかし、日本人が今なお、深い人間関係を求めようとしている傾向があることも事実です。ビジネスでも、お互いによく知り合うために食事やお酒を共にしたり、時にはプライベートな質問をしたりする背景には、こうした「縁」を大切にしようという伝統があるのです。

　また、「縁」には人の力ではどうしようもない定が作用していると仏教では教えます。

　昔から、人に良くすれば、それは必ず自分の未来、また遠い将来生まれ変わった自分に返ってくるという発想があり、過去、あるいは前世の所行によって導かれる人との出会いや関係が「縁」という言葉で表されるのです。

　「縁」は、人との関係を大切にしなければならないという、仏教によって生み出された倫理であり、道徳的な概念ともいえるのです。

Relationships

En describes the concept of a relationship, from first meeting to farewell, and the bond that is developed **therein**.

En is also a word used in Buddhism, meaning the relationships that are created by the Buddha as he brings one person together with another.

There is a phrase in Japanese that "**even a chance encounter is preordained**." This means that all relationships are important and must be taken good care of. The ideal is to treat each person with respect and make the utmost effort to maintain *wa* ("harmony").

Unfortunately, in today's global business culture, there seems to be a trend towards treating relationships as less important. However, it is a fact that the Japanese continue to place a great deal of importance on relationships. Even in business, the tradition of *en* remains alive as people get to know each other better by eating and drinking together, and on occasion, asking personal questions as well.

It is taught in Buddhism that one cannot change the *en* in one's life. This concept is called *sadame.*

Since olden times in Japan, there is the belief that if a person treats others well, that that good will return to him in the future of this life or in a life yet to come. The relationships that a person has formed through one's acts in the past of this life or an earlier life are called *en*.

En is a moral concept, grown out of Buddhist ethics, which emphasizes the importance of human relationships.

仏縁

「仏縁」は、次項で説明する「輪廻」という仏教の教えとも深く関わった概念です。

自らの運命は、前世での行いに大きく左右されていると仏教では教えます。それが「縁」という考え方から育まれる倫理観となっていることは、「縁」の項目で既に解説しました。

「仏縁」とは、自分がすでに忘れた前世や遠い過去での行いがもとで、その人に予定された人との出会いであり、そこで発展する人や社会との関係を意味しています。それは、個人の努力によっては変えられない、ある種の運命といっても過言ではありません。

「仏縁」という考え方が因習となり、封建時代のみならず、つい最近まで、日本社会での差別の原因ともなっていたこともここで強調しなければなりません。すなわち、体が不自由であったり、身分が低く卑しいとされていた人間は、その過去の行いに問題があったとして、偏見の対象となっていたからです。

残念ながら、全ての価値観には良い面と悪い面とがあります。

「仏縁」が善行を行うべきであるという考え方を育む一方で、差別の原因ともなったことの背景には、厳しい身分制度のあった封建時代に、その制度を維持する道具として、「仏縁」が利用されてきたことに起因します。

そして、この考え方は、今でも日本人の心理に影響を与えています。たとえば会社を解雇されたり、上司から不当に扱われても、日本人は欧米ほど激しく争わないようです

Buddha's Fate

Butsuen is a concept with a **deep connection to** the Buddhist teaching of *rinne* ("reincarnation"), which we will discuss in the next chapter.

It is taught in Buddhism that what one did in one's past life greatly affects one's fate in this life. In the last chapter, we already discussed how the concept of *en* has its roots in **ethics**.

Butsuen is the process by which one meets a person based on what one did in an already-forgotten previous life, and then through that person, one develops other relationships in society. **It is not too much to say that** this is a form of fate which can not be changed by the efforts of any person.

It is necessary to emphasize here that, from feudal times right up until recently, the convention of *butsuen* has also been the cause of **discrimination** in Japan. In other words, those who had a physical handicap or a lowly position in society were said to be paying a price for **deeds** in a past life, and they faced discrimination because of that belief.

Unfortunately, all social values have bad aspects as well as good.

The fact that, despite the good it generated, *butsuen* was also the cause of such discrimination, lies in the strict **caste system** of the feudal period, which used *butsuen* as a tool to enforce the system.

Even today, this way of thinking influences the way the Japanese look at things. For example, even if a Japanese loses his job or is treated unfairly by his boss, he tends to look at this as

縁

が、その背景には、こうした運命論による諦めという感覚
が、長年にわたって日本人の中に培われてきたからかもし
れないのです。

輪廻

　「仏縁」という考え方と直接つながる概念が「輪廻」で
す。

　生きるものは全て宇宙の定め、そして「仏」の定めに従
って、さまざまな生き物に生まれ変わり、**生死を繰り返し
てゆく**という考え方が「輪廻」の考え方です。

　仏教のふるさとであるインドなどでも、この考え方は古
くから人々に影響を与えてきました。そして、「輪廻」と
いう概念は仏教の伝来と共に、日本にも深く根をおろした
のです。

　「輪廻」とは過去から未来へとつながる生命の流れであ
り、来世でも幸福な人間として生を受けられるようにとい
う、期待を人々の間に育みました。

　現在の日本では、この考えをそのまま信じている人はほ
とんどいないでしょう。しかし、日本人に来世観がなくな
ったかといえば、そうではありません。人は死後も魂とな
って、**子孫**のもとに現れ、時には子孫を守ってゆくものと
漠然と期待する日本人は今でも多いはずです。

　また、現世で良い行いをすれば、それはどこかで必ず**報
われる**はずだという期待は、今でも多くの日本人の心の奥
底にあるはずです。

　日本に、死者を敬い、その魂を大切にしようとするため

186

fate and does not fight the situation the way a Westerner would.

Reincarnation

The concept of *rinne* is directly related to *butsuen* ("Buddha's fate").

In *rinne,* all living things follow the laws of the universe and the Buddha, being born into this world in one form, dying, and then being reborn in another form **in a never-ending cycle**.

In the home of Buddhism, India, this way of thinking has influenced people since ancient times. Later on Buddhism brought the concept of *rinne* to Japan, where it also became deeply rooted in the society.

Rinne is the transition of life that links the past with the future, giving each person the hope that he will be happy in his next life.

In present-day Japan, there may be few people who believe in *rinne* per se. That said, it is not true that the Japanese do not believe in a future life. There are many Japanese who continue to hold a vague belief that one's spirit is present after death and that that spirit remains near one's **descendants**, protecting then at times.

Deep in the hearts of many Japanese is also the expectation that good deeds done in this life will be **rewarded** in a future life.

The concepts of *rinne* and *butsuen* ("Buddha's fate") can also

のお祭りや、仏教行事が多くあるのも、こうした「輪廻」や「仏縁」という考え方と無関係ではないのです。

因果

「因果」はあらゆるものには原因があり、それによって結果が定められるという仏教の考え方です。

そして、「因果」は、**因果応報**という熟語で頻繁に使われる概念です。

仏縁の項目で説明したように、仏教には前世の悪行や善行によって人の運命が定められるという運命論があり、前世が原因であれば、現在の運命はその結果ということになり、それが「因果」という考え方となっているのです。

「因果応報」とは、単に前世と現在との関係にとどまらず、一生の間でも、自らがなした事柄は必ず自分に返ってくるという教えに基づいた言葉です。たとえば、若い頃に親不孝をして、その後自分が親になったときに自らの子どもに苦しめられることがあったとすれば、それは**典型的な**「因果応報」となります。

また、罪を犯して逃げられたとしても、後に重い病にかかって苦しみ死んでゆくケースがあったとすれば、それも「因果応報」です。

「因果応報」は、いま自らを見舞っている災難や苦しみには、必ずその原因が存在するという考え方なのです。

原因と結果とを示す「因果」という考え方は、「仏縁」や「輪廻」という考え方とも関連し、「縁」という価値観を支える大切な概念となっているのです。

be seen in festivals and Buddhist ceremonies where the dead are honored and their spirits treated with importance.

Cause and Effect

Inga expresses the Buddhist belief that for every cause there is an effect.

Related to *inga* is the often used phrase of *inga ōhō* ("**as a man sows, so shall he reap**").

As we saw in the last chapter on *rinne* ("reincarnation"), the good or bad that a person does in a past life will determine his fate in his next life; in other words, the causes of the last life will result in the effects of the next. This is *inga*.

The phrase *inga ōhō* is not limited to the cause and effect of one's past life on the present; one's deeds in this life will also come back to affect one's fate in this life. For example, if one does not take proper care of one's parents, then one may not receive proper care from one's own children. This would be a **classic case** of *inga ōhō*.

Another case of *inga ōhō* would be someone committing a crime and escaping, but later becoming seriously ill and dying.

In the concept of *inga ōhō*, it is believed that there is always an earlier cause for the difficulties or pains that one may be suffering now.

It may be said that *inga* is closely related to the concepts of *butsuen* ("Buddha's fate") and *rinne* ("reincarnation"), and that it supports the broader social value of *en* ("relationship").

無縁

　最近日本で無縁死という言葉が社会問題として取り上げられました。家族や社会との絆を失ったまま、孤独に死んでゆく老人のことを指した言葉です。

　「和」を保ち、共同体の中で生きてゆくことをよしとしてきた日本人にとって、人との絆が断たれた「無縁」な状態は、日本人が最も恐れることかもしれません。

　現代社会の歪みの中で、孤独な老人が増え、中には親族とも離れさびしく死を迎える人がでてきていることは、日本の新たな現実であるともいえましょう。日本は、組織や集団での共同意識を大切にする反面、以前は顕著であった**家族の絆**は急速に失われつつあります。

　また、若い世代では、そうした伝統的な組織に対する価値観にも無関心で、個人のニーズを社会のニーズよりも優先する若者も増えています。

　こうした新しい世代の影響に加え、現代社会はますます不安定になり、家族、親族とのつながりはどんどん弱くなり、夫婦、兄弟だけの**核家族化**が進んでいるのです。

　「無縁」という言葉は価値観ではないかもしれません。しかし、「無縁」な個人が日本に増えつつあることは、日本の伝統的な価値観に少なからぬ変化が起きていることを示す社会現象であるといえそうです。

Without Ties

Recently in Japan there has been much talk about *muen shi*, "death without ties," or in other words, older people who have lost their ties to family and society and who die alone.

For the Japanese, who place such a priority on maintaining *wa* ("harmony") within a group, the breaking of such ties may be the one thing they fear most.

In today's unstable society, Japan is facing a new reality, where the number of older people living alone is increasing and where many of those people die alone, away from their families. While the Japanese still place a good deal of importance on ties to organizations and groups, the **bond with family**, which had been such a striking feature of Japanese society, continues to weaken.

With the younger generation, all such ties seem to be of less importance, as individual needs are placed before the needs of the society as a whole.

As a result of this influence of the younger generation and the increasing instability of the society as a whole, there has been a trend towards more emphasis on the **nuclear family**—husband and wife and siblings—with weaker ties to the extended family.

The phenomenon of *muen* may not be considered a societal value as such. However, the increasing number of people who experience *muen* is an **indicator** of how some of the basic values of Japanese society are changing.

11

信

Trust

信

　「信」とは信ずることから生まれる固い絆や**安定した関係**を示す言葉です。

　「信」という漢字を分解すれば、左の部分は「人」を意味し、右の部分は「言葉」を意味しています。すなわち、言葉によって**約定**された人と人との強い信頼関係が「信」となります。

　信頼を築く方法はさまざまです。たとえばアメリカでは、信頼の証は、**まっすぐに相手の目を見ること**と固い握手でしょう。そうすることで、相手が何も隠さず、正直に話していると感じられるのです。

　では日本での信頼の証はどうでしょうか。相手の目を強く見つめず、相手に配慮して婉曲にものをいい、時には本音をあえてしゃべらずに、謙遜して自らの望みや実力も誇示しないことが相手から信頼されるコツかもしれません。

　こうしてみると、二つの異なった文化に生きる人同士では、同じ「信」の概念を大切にするにしても、その表現のしかたは正反対ということになります。これは、ある意味ではとても危険なことと言えましょう。

　言葉さえ通じれば、人はみな同じという考え方がいかに深刻な誤解の原因になるかということは、この「信」という概念に対する行動様式の違いをみると明白です。

Trust

Shin refers to a strong and **stable** bond established between two or more people.

If one breaks down the Chinese character for *shin*, one will see that the left side means "person," while the right side means "speak." In other words, the speech exchanged between people become the **promises** which result in a strong relationship of trust.

Trust may be gained in different ways. For example, Amcricans try to gain trust by **looking directly into the other person's eyes** and making a strong handshake. By doing this, it is felt that one is making his thoughts clear, without hiding anything.

In Japan, on the other hand, it may be said that trust is gained by being modest and not putting one's desires first, by being sensitive to the other person's position and speaking in an indirect manner as necessary, and by not looking into the other person's eyes in too aggressive a manner.

In this way, we can see that while both cultures have their own way of expressing trust, they are in fact completely the opposite of each other. This can be a dangerous thing.

It is clear from this discussion about *shin* how serious misunderstandings can occur by assuming that people are the same simply if they can speak each other's language.

信用

　「信用」とは、人と人との**信頼関係**を意味する言葉で、相手を信頼してビジネスを共にし、行動を共にできると判断することを「信用する」といいます。経済的な用語としての「信用」は、相手に**支払い能力**があることを示す言葉でもあります。

　経済的な意味での「信用」はさておき、日本人が相手を「信用する」ポイントは、まず同じグループの「内」の人間であるとお互いに認め合うことに尽きるでしょう。

　たとえば、欧米では見知らぬ者同士が共に仕事をはじめる場合、まず何をおいても一緒に働き出し、そのプロセスの中で結果がよければお互いに信頼関係が**生まれてきます**。それが不安な場合は、まず**契約を結び**、それに拘束される形でお互いに仕事をはじめ、仕事を完成させる中でより深い信頼関係ができあがるのです。

　それに対して、日本の場合は、まずお互いをよく知ることが求められます。食事を共にしたり、時にはお酒を飲んだりしながら、相手がどのような人かを理解し、お互いを「内」の人間と意識できるように努力しつつ、信頼関係を醸成しながらビジネスへと入ってゆくのです。

　最初に契約書というケースは少なく、ビジネスを進めるプロセスの中で必要ならば確認の意味で**覚え書き**にサインする程度なのです。

　したがって、ビジネスの世界でも、日本人は欧米人に比べてより相手のプライベートな情報を聞きたがります。年齢にはじまって、結婚しているかどうか、子どもは何歳で何人いるかなど。お互いに情報を共有し、「内」へと呼び寄せ合うプロセスが必要になるのです。

Credibility

Shin'yō means having a **relationship of trust** with someone, a relationship where one feels at ease doing business or undertaking other activities with that person. The word *shin'yō* ("credit" in this case) is also used in the economic sense to indicate someone's **trustworthiness to make payment**.

Putting the economic sense of *shin'yō* aside for the moment, it may be said that the starting point for trust between two Japanese is to confirm that they are *uchi* ("inside") the same group.

In the West, two people may begin to work together even if they don't know each other well; trust is built up while working together, and that trust is **validated** if the results are good. If there is uncertainty about trust, Westerners will **put a contract in place** and build up trust while completing the project under the terms of the contract.

On the other hand, it is important for Japanese to first know each other well. By dining together, by sometimes drinking together, they will get to know each other, and from there develop trust to the point that they feel they can consider each other as an "insider" (*uchi no mono*). Contracts may not be used much at first; when necessary, a "**memo of understanding**" may be signed to clarify certain aspects of the working relationship.

Because of this approach to trust, it is common for a Japanese to ask many more questions about a person's private life than a Westerner would ask. As part of the process of bringing someone into the "inner" (*uchi*) circle, questions may be asked about a person's age, his marital status, the number of

信

「信用」をまず契約書で保証し、人と人との本来の信頼関係は仕事の結果生まれるとされる欧米社会と、お互いを「内」に取り込み、「情」をもって仕事ができるようにすることが「信用」への最初のプロセスである日本との違いは大きいようです。

信心

「信心」とは宗教的に敬虔であることを示す言葉で、「信心深い」といえば、非常に**強い信仰**をもっていることを示します。

面白いことに、キリスト教やイスラム教では、**一つの絶対神**に対して人々は信仰を持ちます。しかし、神道と仏教の融合がみられるように、一般の日本人はその時々でさまざまな神や仏に対して祈りを捧げます。結婚式はキリスト教の教会で行い、年始には神社にお参りにいき、お盆とでは仏教式にしたがって祖先へのお祈りをします。こうした信仰の受け入れ方は、日本人の「信心」の特徴といえましょう。

日本では、こうした**年中の行事**をしっかりとこなし、神道にも仏教にも常に敬意を表した生活を行っている人のことを「信心深い」といいます。

神道は、さまざまな神がいる多神教。英語では多神教をpolytheismといい、神道を説明するには便利な言葉といえる。これに対して、一神教はmonotheismとなる。

仁

「仁」という漢字を「信」と同じように分解すると、左側

children he has, and so on.

There does appear to be a large difference between these two approaches to trust, with Westerners relying on the guarantees of a contract and the results of the work, while the Japanese rely more on *jō* ("feelings") and the trust developed through the process of vetting someone as worthy of being an "insider."

Faith

Shinjin indicates piety in a religious sense. If one is described as *shinjin bukai*, it means that one has a very **strong belief** in something.

It is interesting to note that Christians and Muslims believe in **one almighty god**, while the Japanese, who follow both Shintō and Buddhist practices, pray to numerous gods. A Japanese may get married in a Christian church, attend a Shintō shrine at New Year, and pray to his ancestors in Buddhist ceremonies during *obon* in the summer. This may be said to be a unique feature of the Japanese version of "faith" (*shinjin*).

In Japan, people who closely follow all of the **annual rites** in both Shintō and Buddhism are said to be *shinjin bukai* ("have a deep faith").

Benevolence

If we break down the Chinese character for *jin* in the same way

信

が「人」、右側が「二」で、人が二人という意味になります。人が二人になったとき、お互いのことを意識し、相手にどのように対応するか考えます。つまり、そこに社会というものが生まれるのです。

「仁」とは、その人と人との接し方、社会での振る舞い方の知恵と愛情を示す言葉で、古代中国の儒教の**根本概念**を現す漢字として日本にも伝わりました。

古代、国を治めるには、社会においては「上」を敬い、「下」を慈しみ、家庭においては父母に「孝」を尽くし、隣人を大切にしてゆくような社会をつくることが必要とされました。「仁」は、そうした考えを示す言葉です。

朱熹などによる新たな儒教は、Neo Confucianismと呼ばれ、日本では「朱子学」などと訳される。江戸時代の為政者に利用され、国の基本を示す学問とまでされたのが朱子学だが、元は人の自然なありかたを見つめたもので、後世のものとかなり異なっていた。

儒教は、日本に伝来して以来、支配階級の規律や心得の哲学として取り入れられ、日本人の道徳律に大きな影響を与えてきました。特に江戸時代にその影響は強く、儒教の一派である**朱子学**が身分制度を維持する思想的背景として取り入れられ、徳川幕府の基本理念となりました。

「仁」をしっかりと心得、実践する人が「信」に足る、すなわち「信用」できる人として尊敬されたのです。

儒教の始祖である孔子の言葉をまとめた論語に、「**巧言令色、鮮なし仁**」という有名な言葉があります。これは言葉が巧みで、愛想のよい表情をする人間ほど、思いやりや慈しみの心が少ないものだという意味の格言です。

この言葉からも理解できるように、日本人が**寡黙**であることを美徳とする背景には、儒教の影響も強くあるのです。

that we did for *shin*, we will see that the left side of *jin* is the character for "person," while the right side is the character for "two." When two people get together, each is aware of the other person and must consider how to deal with that person. In other words, this is where this phenomenon we call "society" begins.

The concept of *jin* came to Japan from China early on as one of the **basic tenets** of Confucianism, denoting this interaction between people as knowledge and love are exchanged.

In ancient times, in order to maintain stability throughout the country, those above oneself were respected, those below were cherished, in the home **filial piety** was observed with one's parents, and one took good care of one's neighbors. *Jin* reflects the values inherent in these actions.

After arriving in Japan, Confucianism became an important part of the moral code and philosophy of the ruling class, and subsequently came to have a large influence over the ethics of all Japanese. This influence was particularly strong during the Edo Period, when the teachings of the **Shushi school of Confucianism** were used to support the strict class system of the Tokugawa government.

Those who actually lived their lives in keeping with the practices of *jin* were respected as people who could be trusted.

There is a famous saying by Confucius: "**The man of flowery speech knows little about benevolence.**" What this means is that the more skilled a person is **in flowery speech**, the less sincere he is in his heart about the needs and feelings of others.

These words reflect again the strong influence of Confucianism in the importance the Japanese ascribe to the virtue of **taciturnity**.

仁義

　「仁」を実践するには、人と人との約束事、すなわち「義」を**大切**にしなければなりません。「義」とはすでに解説した「義理」に通じる考え方と思えばいいでしょう。

　この二つの漢字を合わせると「仁義」となり、人と人との約束事をしっかりと守ることの大切さを説く熟語となるのです。

　もちろん、「仁義」は武士などの支配階級では「忠義」という言葉に置き換えられ、大切な価値観として尊重されました。

　そして、庶民レベルでは、友人との約束や、人から与えられた「恩」に対してありがたく思うことが、「仁義」と**解釈**されてきました。そういう意味で、「仁義」は、やくざの世界などでは特に重んじられ、親分と子分との間の「仁義」をめぐる葛藤などは、今でも映画の題材として取り上げられています。

　言い換えれば、「仁義」を守ることが「信」につながり、「信」を得るためには、「仁義」に厚い心を持つことが大切です。

　「内」と意識した人間へは、その人を**裏切**らないように、「仁義」がうまれます。相手に対して「仁義」を感じることが、相手への「情」にもつながるのです。

Moral Code

In order to be a person of benevolence (*jin*), one must **honor** one's *gi* ("commitments"). In this case, *gi* is the same Chinese character used in *giri* ("obligations"), which we discussed earlier, and the two words have the same basic meaning.

If we combine the characters for *jin* and *gi*, we get *jingi,* which, as we noted above, denotes the importance of honoring one's commitments.

Among the ruling classes, the word *chūgi* ("loyalty") could be substituted for *jingi*. *Chūgi* was of course a particularly important value for the ruling classes.

Among the common people, on the other hand, *jingi* **was interpreted as** the promises kept among friends or the *on* ("social debt") that had been incurred with someone. *Jingi* in this sense is an especially important value for the yakuza, and there are even now many movies made where the central theme is complications in the commitments between a yakuza boss and his underling.

Putting it another way, honoring one's moral code (*jingi*) engenders trust (*shin*), and in turn trust strengthens one's commitment to one's moral code.

In order to not **betray** those who are in one's inner circle (*uchi*), one must have *jingi*. Having a sense of *jingi* means that one also has a sense of affection (*jō*) for those with whom one interacts.

12

徳

Virtue

徳

　「徳」とは、日本人の価値観に精通し、それを実践し、そのことによって世の中にも必要とされる知性を指します。

　したがって、「徳」のある人とは、人から尊敬され、何か必要なことがあれば、その人の意見を求め、時にはその人に教えを請います。

　では、徳のある人物とはどのような人物像でしょうか。

　まず、なんといってもその人は「謙譲」の精神をもって、常に控えめで、自分をアピールすることなど決してありません。腰が低く、「情」と「義理」とをよく理解しています。

　その人は、**しかも「道」を極めた「匠」**かもしれません。しかし、すでに世の中の酸いも甘いも知り尽くし、厳しさよりも、穏やかさをもって人を包み込むような人かもしれません。

　「徳」のある人は、人生の達人で、**決して堅物ではありません**。礼儀作法をしっかりと嗜み、道徳をよく心得ながらも、楽しむことにかけても達人です。日本人の知恵や価値観を**集約した知恵**。それが「徳」の意味するところなのです。

名

　「名」とは、人の表の顔です。元々「名」は人の名前のことで、その人にとって最も大切なアイデンティティとなります。

　そして「名」は、その人にとっての名誉、そして地位を

Virtue

The principle of *toku* ("virtue") is known and practiced by the Japanese, and through *toku* one learns what is necessary to be wise.

People of virtue are respected, and when necessary, a person will seek out their opinion or ask that they serve as a teacher.

What type of a person would we describe as being virtuous?

First, such a person is *kenjō* ("modest"), never seeking to blindly promote his own interests. He also has a good understanding of *jō* ("feelings") and *giri* ("obligation").

Furthermore, such a person may have the *takumi* ("skill") to "**take the road (*michi*) as far as it will go.**" But it is also true that such a person may have already reached a point where he is confident and settled, and is neither bitter nor naive about life.

A **virtuous person** has mastered life, and **knows how to adjust to its twists and turns**. He is also a master of being able to enjoy life, following proper etiquette with grace while maintaining an ethical spirit. Being able to **integrate** wisdom with principle—this is the definition of *toku*.

Name

Na ("name") is the **outward representation of a person's face**. The root meaning of *na* is "name," an essential aspect of a person's identity.

Na also refers to a person's honor and position. When a

も意味します。社会的に**しっかりとした**地位を築いたとき、人はあの人は「**名を成した**」といいます。そして一般的に「名」を成した人は、「徳」をも備えていることが期待されます。

「名」を成すということは、出世し人々から尊敬される人のことですから、そのことによって、その人は、**外見上**は少なくとも名誉を勝ち得たことになります。そのような人にとって名誉を維持することはとても重要です。名誉とは、**精神的に高潔であること**と、社会的に認められことの二つの側面を持ちますが、時にはその二つは**矛盾する**こともあります。武士にとっては、精神的に高潔であることが本当の名誉とされていたのですが、現実はというと、やはり人間は弱い者で、表面上の社会的地位を維持することによって、「名」を維持してきた人が多いようです。

「名」を維持することが、もし、何らかの理由で困難になったとき、その名は「恥」で汚されることになります。

恥

「義理」の項で紹介したルース・ベネディクトは、『菊と刀』で、西欧での「罪」の意識と対応する日本人の価値観として「恥」の意識を取り上げ、話題となった。

「名」は「恥」と表裏一体の価値観です。

「恥」とは、単に恥ずかしいことではなく、自らが大切にする「名」を**汚す**ことによって損なわれる名誉心を意味する言葉です。

欧米の人は、キリスト教的な倫理観にそぐわない行為をしたときに、「罪」の意識を感じるといわれています。それに対して日本人は、「罪」ではなく「恥」の意識を抱くわけです。

person has built a **solid** position for himself in society, that person is said to have "**established a name**" (*na wo nashita*). It is expected that such a person will be virtuous.

A person who has established his name (*na*) is respected by people, meaning that, at least for **outward appearances**, he has earned a certain degree of honor and prestige. For such a person, it is very important that he maintain his honor. There are two aspects to honor: the **internal integrity** that one maintains and the external recognition that comes from society. Sometimes these two aspects of honor can be **in conflict** with each other. For the samurai, internal integrity was supposed to be the true definition of honor, but being human, it seems that in many cases, the external recognition of society was just as important, if not more so.

Maintaining one's *na* becomes difficult if, for some reason, one stains one's name with *haji* ("shame").

Shame

Haji ("shame") is the opposite side of *na* ("name").

Haji is not simply doing something embarrassing; it means **staining** one's name and thereby losing one's honor.

It is said that Westerners will view an act that is contrary to the ethics of their Christian moral law as a **sin**. Rather than sin, the Japanese are concerned with *haji* ("shame").

　「恥」とは、**内省的に**自らに問いかけて恥ずかしく思う他に、共同体の他の人々に対して恥ずかしく思うという意識もついてきます。常に他とのバランスの中で、自らが特に過ちなどを犯して**特異な状況**になることに対して、人は「恥」の意識をもつのです。

　たとえば、死を畏れて戦いから**逃げて**しまった武士がいるとして、その武士は自らの弱い心を見つめて恥じ入るのと同時に、家族や同僚や同郷の人々、そして自らが仕える君主に対して「恥」の念を持ちます。

　また、儒教的な観点からは、先祖に対して恥ずかしく思うといったように、祖先、時には子孫への「恥」という多面的な意識を抱くのです。

　確かに、「和」を重んずるせいか、日本人は自らが行動するとき、常に他人のこと**を気にする**傾向にあります。他人と異なる行動をするとき、多かれ少なかれ日本人は「恥」の意識と戦わなければならず、それを克服して自らの意思を通してゆくための**勇気**が要求されるのです。

面目

　よく中国人は面子を大切にするといいます。

　その人の立場を尊重し、その人の体裁を傷つけないようにすることを、中国の人は「**その人の面子を守る**」といいます。

　日本にも面子の概念も面目という言葉も存在します。

As well as an **introspective** questioning of oneself, the concept of *haji* also involves how one is viewed by the surrounding community. One must always maintain one's balance with others, seeking to avoid making a mistake that will put one **at odds** with the community and result in *haji*.

For example, if during a battle a soldier were to **desert** his unit out of fear, he would not only have to come to terms with himself about his shameful act, he would also have to deal with the *haji* he had brought on his family, his comrades, his country, and if he were a samurai, the lord he was serving.

As in Confucian thought, the concept of avoiding *haji* extends to one's grandparents and can also include one's grandchildren.

Most likely due to the importance placed on maintaining *wa* ("harmony"), the Japanese tend to always **be concerned about** what others will think. Whenever the Japanese do something different from what most other people would do, even if it is not significantly different, they must find the **courage** to battle and overcome their feelings of *haji*.

Face

It is often said that the Chinese place a great deal of importance on "face."

In other words, the Chinese "**save face**" when a person's position is respected, and nothing is done which would harm that person's social standing.

The Japanese have a similar concept of "face" (*menboku* or

徳

そして同じ意味をもって、それを「面目」という言葉で表明することが多いようです。自らの名誉を大切にし、自らの名に恥じないよう気をつかってゆくことを、人は「面目を保つ」というのです。

　日本人は、「**面目**」が**潰れた**とき、「恥」を意識し、「面目」が潰れる原因をつくった人に対して怒りを覚えます。

　たとえば、会議で上司が自分の意見を言ったとき、部下がそれに反論すると、上司は「面目」を潰されます。ですから、部下は上司の体裁を保つために、その場では強く反論せずに、後で別の「場」をもって上司に自らの考えを伝えるのです。

　そうした意味で、「面目」という価値観は、「和」や「場」、そして「間」などの概念とも深く関連しているのです。

　人前で自らの意見を表明することを悪いこととは思わない欧米の**価値観**と、この「面目」という価値観は鋭く対立します。日本人にとって、「面目」とは相手の立場を考え、相手に「恥」をかかさないように「配慮」することの大切さを教える価値観です。相手の気持ちになって物事を考えれば、自然と「面目」は保たれ、人との「和」が維持できるのです。

mentsu). One must "protect one's face" (*menboku wo tamotsu)* by taking care of one's honor and ensuring that one's name is not stained with *haji* ("shame").

A Japanese person will feel shame if he **loses face**, and he will be angry with the person or people who have caused him such shame.

For example, if a person were to openly oppose his boss during a meeting, the boss would lose face. In order to avoid this, the subordinate in this case would seek a different *ba* ("place") to present his views to his boss.

In this sense, the concept of *menboku* is closely related to the concepts of *wa* ("harmony"), *ba* ("place"), and *ma* ("space").

The concept of *menboku* tends to conflict sharply with the **norms** of Westerners, for whom voicing one's opinion in front of others is not a bad thing. For the Japanese, on the other hand, it is important to always consider the position of others and ensure that no *haji* ("shame") is brought to them. If one keeps the feelings of others in mind, *menboku* ("face") will be saved without making any special efforts, and *wa* ("harmony") will be maintained.

分

　「分」とは日本に古くからあるその人の立場にあった言動を期待する価値観です。昔は身分の低い者には身分に応じた「分」があり、たとえば身分の高い人の司る領域に口をはさみ、意見をいうことはタブーでした。そうした行為は、「**分をわきまえない行為**」とされ、厳しく追及されたのです。

　現在では「分」は、自らの社会的地位や会社での上下関係などの中に織り込まれた価値観となっています。

　新入社員は自らの「分」を守って、「先輩」に敬意を表し、上司の指示に黙って従いながら、仕事を学びます。学校でのクラブ活動では、下級生は上級生が活動する場所を掃除し、言葉遣いも丁寧にし、それぞれの立場での「分」に従った練習することが期待されます。

　この「分」を逸脱した行動をした場合、相手の「**面目**」を**潰す**ことになるのです。

　縦社会の典型のように思われるこの「分」という概念が、今なお日本人の心の中に生きていることには驚かされます。

　全ての人は平等であると規定されている現代社会においての「分」という考え方。それは、お互いに摩擦なく相手を尊重して組織や社会の「和」を維持するための暗黙の**了解**とでもいえそうです。

Role

The principle of *bun* concerns the "role" that a person was expected to play based on his position in society. In the old days, it was taboo for a person of low rank to approach or talk to a person of high rank. This was known as *bun wo wakimaeru* ("**understanding one's role**"), and such practices were strictly enforced.

Today the principle of *bun* is still commonly found in the *jōge* ("hierarchy") relationships, which one maintains according to one's social position.

For a young person just joining a company, he will play his *bun* by respecting his *senpai* ("seniors") and obediently following their directions in learning his job. In clubs at school as well, it is expected that each person will play his *bun*, with the newer, more junior students using polite language towards the older, more senior students, while also doing chores such as cleaning up after them.

When a person does not properly play his *bun*, he may "**do damage**" to the "**face**" of another.

It is surprising that this concept of *bun*, which may be thought of as typical of a classical "**vertical society**," is still alive now in the hearts of Japanese.

In today's society, where all people are expected to be treated equally, it can be said that the **implicit consent** behind the concept of *bun* contributes to the overall *wa* ("harmony") maintained in companies and other organizations.

阿吽の呼吸
あ うん

Intuitiveの名詞であるIntuitionは「直感」を意味する。もともと阿吽とは、サンスクリット語で、阿が口を開き、吽が口を閉じて声を出すこと。狛犬の片方が口を開け、片方が口を閉じていることも阿吽に起因する。阿吽そのものが呼吸を表し、一対の狛犬のように直感的に意図を相手に伝えることが、阿吽の呼吸の由来。

ここに記してきた日本人の価値観に支えられたさまざまなコミュニケーションスタイルを使いこなすことによって、相手にあえてすべてを語らなくても意思疎通ができる状態を「阿吽の呼吸」といいます。

たとえば、相手の立場を理解して、自らの「分」をわきまえれば、口に出して説明しなくても、その「場」での言動はコントロールできます。

「和」の精神が理解でき、「型」を心得ていれば、あえて人に対してその行為について**詳細を質問する必要もありません**。

すなわち、こうしたプロトコルがわかっていれば、言葉を少なくしても、相手に**意思や意図**を伝えることができるのです。

言葉を交わさなくても、即座に相手の意図が理解でき、その期待に合致した行動がとれる間柄、すなわち「阿吽の呼吸」の間柄こそ、「内」の関係であり、本音で話せる親しい関係といえましょう。

ある研究によると、日本人は欧米の人に比べて、言葉の行間の意味を理解し、より簡単に文脈で意思疎通ができるということです。しかし、この発想は、日本人同士の価値観に基づいた交流を理解できない欧米の人にとっては誤解の原因となります。

Intuitive Communication

For the Japanese, who with their shared social values are able to use a variety of methods to communicate, getting one's point across with a limited amount of words is known as *aun no kokyū* (literally, "breathing in harmony").

For example, if one understands the position of the person one is dealing with, and one is able to properly play one's *bun* ("role"), then one will be able to control the flow of the conversation of that particular setting and it will not be necessary to use many words.

If one understands the spirit of *wa* ("harmony") and the *kata* ("form") of the moment, it will not be necessary to **ask detailed questions** about what is happening.

In other words, if this type of "protocol" is followed, a person will be able to express his **intent** with a minimum of words.

It is precisely this type of relationship, where one is able to have one's intent immediately understood by the other person without the use of words, which the Japanese would describe as *aun no kokyū*.

Studies done in the past show that, compared to Westerners, the Japanese are able to fill in meanings based on context more easily. This can lead to misunderstanding on the part of Westerners who are unfamiliar with this type of communication used between Japanese.

礼

　「礼」とは、中国で生まれた儒教の倫理観の中でも最も大切な価値観です。それは社会の**秩序**や**規範**を保ち、人が社会をつくってゆくために必要な**規律**や、**道徳**を表す言葉です。

　すなわち「礼」を心得るということは、世の中の仕組みの奥にある価値観を理解し、人と人との関係を構築してゆく知恵を持っているということになります。

　そして、中国から多くの倫理観を輸入しながらも、日本の風土の中で日本向けに運用してきた日本人には、独特の「礼」の捉え方があります。

　日本人にとって、「礼」を知るということは、ここに記したさまざまな日本人の価値観を**習得し**、それをもって人を導き、社会の「和」を保つために運用する知恵をもつということになります。

　すなわち、「礼」を知る人こそ、「徳」のある人であるといえるのです。

　「礼」は、人に感謝の意を表明することも意味し、同時に社会でのマナーを意味する「礼儀」という言葉にも使用されている漢字です。人に敬意を表し、上下の関係を尊重して丁寧に人に対応することが礼儀です。「礼」を心得る人は、当然人に対する礼儀も重んじ、世の中の「義理」にも真摯に対応します。

　社会の規律や価値観を知悉した人は、「阿吽の呼吸」によって人の期待するものを読み取り、人がそれを要求する前に、その期待に対して丁寧に対応をすることができるわ

Etiquette

Rei ("etiquette") is a very important value born out of the ethics of Chinese Confucianism. It helps to protect the **order** and **norms** that are necessary to build a society with broadly accepted **discipline** and **ethics**.

In other words, in order to understand *rei*, one must understand the basic social values behind the broader social framework, and from there have the wisdom to build relationships person-by-person.

While the ethical framework of Japanese society was imported from China, the Japanese have adapted the concept of *rei* to their own ways and developed their own unique version.

For the Japanese, in order to understand *rei*, one must **grasp** the various social values outlined here, and with those values, one must be able to guide people and maintain *wa* ("harmony") in society.

In other words, a person who understands *rei* is a person who also understands *toku* ("virtue").

Rei means "to give thanks," and it is also the first Chinese character in the word *reigi* (another word for "etiquette"). *Reigi* also means to follow carefully the expectations of *jōge* ("hierarchical") relationships, as well as to treat others politely and with respect. Of course people who understand *rei* and *reigi* are also earnest in taking care of their obligations (*giri*—the *gi* of *giri* being the same character as the *gi* of *reigi*).

Those who fully comprehend discipline and basic values will, through "breathing in harmony," be able to respond politely to people's expectations before being asked. It is said that "**he**

けです。「一を聞いて十を知る」という言葉がありますが、「礼」をわきまえる人は、こうした人の期待に対して多くを語らず、迅速かつ寡黙に応え、しかもその成果を誇示したりはしません。

　日本人にとっての「礼」は、静かな行動の中に自ずとにじみ出る知性といえるのではないでしょうか。

諦観

　「分」という価値観を思い出してください。

　昔から「分」は、身分や上下関係と深く関わった価値観として捉えられてきました。その発想で人間全体を一つのグループとして考えれば、その上にあるものとは神や仏、あるいは宇宙といった、**人知を超えた存在である**ということになります。

　人間は人間である以上、こうした**超越的な存在**に対しても「分」を持ちます。たとえば、人は死を超越できません。また、未来を見通すことや、過去を変えることもできません。

　そんな人間の限界を人間の「分」として捉えることが、人間としての知恵をもった人、すなわち「**徳」のある人**ということになります。

　「諦観」とは、そのまま訳せば「あきらめ」ということになりますが、実際は、何が人間の「分」であるかを心得ることを意味し、その**限界**を知ることを「諦観」と呼んでいるのです。

　従って、知恵ある人、「徳」のある人は、「諦観」を併せ

who hears one knows ten." Those who understand *rei* respond to expectations quickly, with few words, and do not **boast** about what they have done.

For the Japanese, it can be said that *rei* is wisdom that comes naturally from one's quiet actions.

Resignation

Please recall our earlier discussion about the concept of *bun* ("role").

From ancient times, *bun* has been closely related to rank and *jōge* ("hierarchical") relationships. If we think of humans as one group, then in terms of *jōge*, the rank above humans would be a god or gods, space, or something else **beyond human knowledge**.

Humans also have a *bun* ("role") to play in relation to such a **transcendent being**. For example, humans cannot overcome death. Humans also cannot see the future or change the past.

People who understand these limits in a profound sense as the *bun* ("part") to be played by humans may be considered wise; in other words, they are **persons of virtue** (*toku*).

Taken literally, *teikan* means "resignation." However, what *teikan* truly means is the wisdom of understanding human **limitations** and discovering what one's *bun* ("role") should be within those limitations.

It follows that wise and virtuous people will also understand

持っているはずです。

　人が新たなことにチャレンジすることはよいことであるとしながらも、人の存在そのものの限界を理解することによって、より人にやさしく接するというのが「諦観」の持つ美学なのです。

　「礼」という価値を知ることによって、人の社会での知恵を抱き、「諦観」を抱くことによって、より大きな自然や宇宙、そして神や仏の存在に敬意を払うことが、「徳」を磨いた知恵者に求められる**究極の条件**であるといえるのです。

沈黙

　「沈黙」とは、あえて、自らが成し遂げたことをアピールしたり、たとえ自らが間違って批判されても、自らの正当性を強調したりせず、**沈黙する**ことをよしとする美学です。

　これは、自らの道を自力で切り開き、時には自分をしっかり守りながら自分の立場を高めてゆくことをよしとする西欧の人々にとって、最も理解しがたい価値観かもしれません。

　自らの**業績**をアピールする行為は、自分の利益を優先し、「和」を保ち「恩」に報いる行為とは**対立します**。さらに自らの正当性をアピールする行為は、自分の利益を優先するための言い訳ととられ、**嫌われます**。

　時にはあえて非難をも受け入れ、沈黙することによっ

the true meaning of *teikan*.

While it is a good thing to challenge new objectives, one of the virtues of *teikan* is a tendency to treat other people better, which may come from understandings our limitations.

To be recognized as a polished person of virtue and wisdom, the **ultimate requirement** may be that through our understanding of *rei* ("etiquette") and *teikan* ("resignation"), we pay the proper respect to our gods.

Silence

Chinmoku is the virtue of maintaining one's silence instead of promoting oneself; even if one is criticized for being wrong, one **stays silent** instead of trying to explain why one is right.

This may be a very difficult concept to understand for Westerners, who highly value the importance of making one's own way in the world and defending oneself as necessary.

Promoting one's own **accomplishments** and putting one's own interests ahead of those of others are **at odds** with the values of *wa* ("harmony") and working to repay *on* ("social debt"). Making arguments about the correctness of one's position is again seen as trying to put one's interests ahead of others, and **is looked down upon**.

In certain cases, people may in fact **feel more inclined** to

て、人々はむしろその人の正当性を感じ取り、その耐え忍ぶ心の強さに共感してゆくのです。

「沈黙」には強い意志が必要です。従って、すぐに自らの立場を主張し、自らの力量をアピールすることは、日本人が一番大切にする**我慢して「道」を切り開く**というストイックな行為にも反することになるわけです。

実際、日本人は欧米の人よりも寡黙であるといわれます。日本人を前にスピーチなどをした欧米の人は、この沈黙する行為に驚き、日本人が何も聞いていないとか、自分の提案が受け入れられなかったという風に誤解することがあるのです。

こうした寡黙な日本人が期待するもの。それが封建時代から受け継がれてきた社会構造のなかにあって、雄弁に自らをアピールすることなく、ただ黙々と「忠義」を尽くしたり、仕事に励む者に、人々が抱く「情」や「恩」という概念なのです。

潔い
いさぎよ

「謙虚」でない上に、「沈黙」を守れず、自らをアピールし続ける人のことを、日本人は「彼は潔くない」と批判します。

「潔い」という言葉は、無実であることを示す「潔白」、あるいは清らかであることを示す「清潔」などの概念とも結びつきます。すなわち、「潔い」ことは、日本人が最も大切にする**精神的な美学**といえるかもしれません。

もし、事前に傷めたことによる筋肉痛で優勝を逃した陸上選手がいたとします。選手は筋肉痛さえなければ充分

recognize the correctness of a person's position due to his stoic silence.

Chinmoku requires a strong will. For the Japanese, the best way to promote one's own interests and impress people is **through self-restraint and forbearance**, which in turn opens the *michi* ("way") to further development.

Japanese are indeed often said to be more taciturn than Westerners. When speaking before a group of Japanese, Westerners will be surprised at the silence and will mistakenly think that the Japanese are not really listening or that their proposal was not well received.

In this society built on connections and feudal principles, what the so-called "taciturn Japanese" are expecting is respect for the principle of paying back *on* ("social debt") and an affection for those who have made their best efforts to uphold the values of *chūgi*.

Principled

The Japanese will criticize as *isagiyokunai* ("unprincipled") those who are not modest and instead speak out to promote their own interests.

The word *isagiyoi* is linked to the words *keppaku* and *seiketsu*, both of which mean "pure," and therefore by association with the concept of cleanliness. For the Japanese, *isagiyoi* is a very important **spiritual aesthetic**.

Let's assume that there is a runner competing in a track event who knows beforehand that he will not be able to win due

優勝ができる実力があったとしても、インタビューを受けたとき、その選手は筋肉痛を理由にして優勝できなかったとは、決して答えないはずです。むしろ、「まだまだこれが自分の実力なのです」と、言葉少なく語るはずです。

そして、どことなくその選手がケガをしながら頑張ったことが周囲に伝わると、人々は「彼は潔い」と感動し、その選手の**評価**が高まるのです。

伝統的に日本では「潔い」対応をする人物は「高潔なる人」と呼ばれてきました。寡黙で、強い精神力を持つ人物のことを、人はそのように呼ぶのです。こうした人物は、人の話を聞くときも、得てして静かに目を閉じています。または、じっと下を向いて相手の話に聞き入ることもあります。これらの行為は、真剣に「情」をもって相手に接するときにも多く見られる行為なのです。

西欧では、目を閉じたり視線をそらす人は、何かを隠しているのではないかと疑われます。ここに、日本人と欧米の人とのコミュニケーション上での**大きな誤解が生まれ**るのです。

to a pulled muscle. If the runner had not had the pulled muscle, he is confident that he could have won the event, but at the interview after the race, he does not mention the injury. In fact, he instead says that this is "all he is capable of."

Later, when it is found out that the runner did his best despite the injury, people will say that he is *isagiyoi* ("a man of principle"), and his **reputation** will increase.

Traditionally in Japan, one who leads an *isagiyoi* life is said to be a person of *kōketsu* ("high principle"). A taciturn person of strong will would be described in this way. It is common for such people to quietly close their eyes when listening to others. Sometimes they will keep their head bowed motionlessly while listening. By doing this, it can be seen that they are sincerely intent on listening closely to what the other person is saying.

For Westerners, it may appear that a person like this who closes or averts his eyes has something to hide. This sometimes **significant to large misunderstandings** between Japanese and Westerners.

13

美

Beauty

美

　日本の美とはどのようなものでしょうか。

　日本の美を語る上で、際立った四季があることは重要です。日本は**温帯**に位置するため、春夏秋冬、それぞれの季節感が**際立**っています。季節ごとの風物や美術や工芸、さらには日本料理があり、その季節ならではの特長が活かされているのです。

　また、日本人は季節の移ろいに、仏教での「**無常**」を重ね、はかない人生をそこに投影させてきました。日本の古典文学では、このテーマが常に繰り返されています。

　こうした季節感は、日本人を**観念的**なものより、むしろビジュアル的な表現方法へと駆り立てます。

　近世の絵画を代表する浮世絵や、現代の漫画やアニメで、その原点をたどれば、四季折々の風物をただ写生するのではなく、デフォルメして表現してきた伝統に到達します。

　たとえば秋という季節感をいかにして表現するかは、山野の風物をそのまま描くより、**紅葉**を幾葉か組み合わせ、美しい線で描いた方がより鮮明に人々に訴えかけます。

　こうしたデフォルメによるミニマリズムは、古くは禅寺の石庭にはじまり、線と色の組み合わせのみで表現する**浮世絵**や、文芸の世界では短い語句の中に自然や事物への思いを盛り込む俳句などにみられる、日本の芸術の特徴といえましょう。

ミニマリズムは、芸術の上で装飾を極力排して表現する考え方を示し、特に現代美術の中で追求された。英語のMinimalismの元となるMinimalという言葉は「最小の」という意味で、そこからミニマル・デザインやミニマル・ミュージックなどという言葉が生まれた。

*ebb and flow　引き潮と上げ潮

Beauty

What exactly is beauty for the Japanese?

Among other things, it must be said that within the Japanese concept of beauty, the ebb and flow* of the four seasons is very important. Geographically located in a **temperate zone** of the earth, Japan is a country where summer, fall, winter, and spring can all be experienced **to their fullest**. Each season has its own art, its own crafts, and certainly also its own food, each of which reflect the nuances of that particular time of the year.

For the Japanese, too, there is the Buddhist element of *mujō* ("transience"), which adds to the **sense of impermanence** seen in the changing of the seasons. This theme is a common one in classical Japanese literature.

The Japanese tend to express this sense of the seasons more visually than **conceptually**.

Rather than simply sketching the various elements of the four seasons as they appear directly to the eye, a tradition of expressing things in a more indirect manner has developed in modern wood block prints, manga, and anime.

For example, in depicting a fall scene, one may be able to make a deeper impact by drawing the fine lines of **colorful leaves** arranged in a pattern rather than a broader scene of mountains and fields.

It may be said that this type of indirect expression and the minimalism with which it is associated are particular features of Japanese art. Starting in ancient times with the gardens of Zen temples, these features can be seen in the lines and colors of **wood block prints** as well as in the **abbreviated form** of poetry known as *haiku*.

わび

　色とりどりのきらびやかなものより、簡素でひなびたものの中に見いだす美しさを「わび」といいます。

　15世紀、「わび」は茶道などと共に語られるようになった美学で、それは茶器や茶室など目に見えるものだけではなく、無駄を排除し、質素なライフスタイルの中にやすらぎを見いだそうとする禅の発想とも融合して、人々の間に広がりました。

　たとえば、宝石をちりばめた器で美酒を飲むよりも、素焼きのお椀で清水を飲む方が、より味わいがあり、風雅であるというのが「わび」の考え方です。自然の中に自らをおいて、身の回りのものは最低限にし、季節の移ろいを肌で感じることに心の安らぎを得、同時に世の「無常」を思うことができるというのが「わび」の概念です。

　「わび」は、日本人が最も大切にする精神世界でもあり、物欲による贅沢ではなく、精神的な贅沢を求める上での理想であるともいえるのです。

さび

　「わび」と共に、時には対で語られるのが「さび」という概念です。「さび」とは、古くなり劣化したものの中に見いだす美の世界です。

　たとえば、古い日本家屋の廊下などは、時とともに磨かれ風化して木目が見えてきます。そんな家に住めば、夜、雨戸がガタガタと鳴ることによって、冬の前触れである木

The Beauty of the Simple

Wabi is the beauty found in the simple and **desolate**, as opposed to the beauty found in bright colors.

Wabi was a concept that began to emerge as part of the tea ceremony in the 15th century. Over time it spread across Japan not simply in reference to the simplicity of the tea house or the tools of tea, but more broadly in connection with the Zen philosophy of meditation.

For example, *wabi* would dictate that rather than drinking *sake* from a **cup elaborately inlaid with jewels**, it would be more refined to drink spring water from an **unglazed bowl**. *Wabi* might be felt, too, when one is alone, surrounded by nature, observing the changing of the seasons and also sensing the transience of this life.

Wabi is a very important aspect of the Japanese value system, where the ideal is found not in the luxury of things, but rather in the **luxury of the spirit**.

The Beauty of the Decaying

The concept of *sabi* is often spoken of together with the concept of *wabi*. *Sabi* is the beauty found in that which is old and **decaying**.

For example, one might see *sabi* in the worn grain of the polished wood of the corridors of an old Japanese house. And if one were to live in such a house, one might experience *sabi* (or both

枯らしを実感し、その音をじっくり味わいながら俳句をつくるといったことが、「さび」であり、「わび、さび」と一つにして語られる美学なのです。

　また、日本の**仏像**は塗料がはげ落ちても、そのままにされ、現れた古木の美しさの中で微笑む仏像に人々は祈りを捧げます。朽ちてゆくものへの美意識がなければ、造られた当時の彩色を施し、新しく生まれ変わった仏像を安置するはずです。

　実は、質素で古いものをうまく使いこなし、そこから茶道や華道といった様式美が生みだされたことからも理解できるように、「わび」や「さび」の世界はそれを「美」の世界へと高めた**洗練**なのです。

　日本庭園では、よく苔が使われます。

　石を配置するとき、**苔むした石**を置くことで、「さび」の世界を表現しようとするのです。枯山水という庭園では、あえて池を造らず、石と砂と樹木で自然を表現し、石庭では樹木すらおかずに石と砂のみで自然界を表します。

　それは簡素で古くなったもの、つまり「わび、さび」の概念で造られるミニマリズムの世界なのです。

艶
（つや）

　艶とは、**洗練されていること**を示す言葉です。

　「わび、さび」の概念からもわかるように、決して贅沢なものを着こなし、**きらびやかなものの中に身を置くこと**が洗練ではありません。歴史的にみるならば、「わび、さび」は都会人の嗜みでした。こうした一見贅沢に見えない

wabi and *sabi*) in hearing the sound of the night shutters being opened or closed, and hearing those sounds, one might recall the cold of the winter and be moved to write a *haiku* poem.

In Japan, people may be seen praying to old **statues of the Buddha** where the lacquer has fallen off and only the bare wood remains. If there were no such appreciation of the beauty of the decaying, then these old statues would be repainted and restored to their original state.

As can be seen in the tea ceremony and flower arrangement, *wabi* and *sabi* are not only the appreciation of the simple or the old; they also represent the **refinement** of such elements into the realm of "beauty."

Moss is commonly used in Japanese gardens.

Sabi is expressed by using **moss-covered rocks** in the garden. In the style of garden known as *karesansui*, no water is used, and nature is represented only with rocks, sand, and plants; in the style known as *sekitei*, only rocks and sand are used.

This is a minimalist world created with the simple and the old, or in other words, with *wabi* and *sabi*.

Refinement

The word *tsuya* means "**refinement**."

As was seen in our discussion of *wabi* and *sabi*, it is not considered refined to dress oneself up in luxurious and **glittering** clothing. From an historical point of view, we can see how *wabi* and *sabi* came to reflect the **tastes** of city people. Over time, this

おしゃれな感覚は、そのまま時代とともに受け継がれ、庶民の美意識の中にも浸透していったのです。

　江戸時代に、都会ならではの遊女との享楽や色恋が浮世絵や当時の出版物で流布するようになると、おしゃれに遊ぶことが艶なことだとされ、**町人**の間で、さまざまなライフスタイルが流行します。

　特に、当時の為政者が**質素倹約**を法制化したこともあり、贅沢にはさまざまな規制が押し付けられました。そうした中で、表には現れない贅沢さ、そしておしゃれが追求されたのです。元来派手好きな町人は、あえて目に見えないところや、ちょっとしたアクセントに気を配り、贅沢を追求したのです。

　艶とは、「わび、さび」の概念を取り入れながらも、**派手好き**な町人の生命力が融合し、都会的な洗練へと進化した美意識であるといえましょう。

　江戸時代、「艶」のある人といえば、セクシーでおしゃれな人という意味で、庶民のあこがれとなっていたのです。

みやび
雅

　京都は長い間日本の首都として、**宮廷**がおかれていました。

　その千年の歴史の中で培われてきた宮廷文化が醸し出す、**優雅で洗練**された雰囲気を「雅」といいます。

　宮廷やそこに生きる**貴族**によって守られてきた「雅」

"non-luxurious" **stylishness** came to be a part of the sense of beauty held by the common people.

During the Edo era, what was *tsuya* ("refined") came to be influenced by what was going on in the licensed districts. Wood block prints (*ukiyoe*) of dandies with the women of these districts became popular, setting the tone for fashion and other aspects of the daily life of the **townspeople**.

At that time, the authorities had regulations in place to enforce a **frugal lifestyle**, and there were many restrictions on any ostentatious displays of wealth. Given these circumstances, the townspeople were forced to adopt more subtle expressions of luxury and fashion, using an accent here or there in their attire, or even in their under-clothing, which could not be seen.

It may be said that *tsuya* combined the concepts of *wabi* and *sabi* with the townspeople's innate love of the **flashy** to produce the big-city sense of beauty.

During the Edo era, a person who was refined was seen as someone who was fashionable and sexy.

Elegance

As the capital of Japan, Kyoto was the location for the **imperial court** for a very long time.

Over that thousand-year history, the culture of the imperial court developed a **graceful elegance** which in Japanese is called *miyabi*.

The culture of *miyabi* developed by the **nobles** at the

な文化は、浮世絵などに代表される町人文化が醸し出す「艶」と対照的な美意識です。

　15世紀後半から16世紀にかけて、日本は戦国時代となり、当時京都にあった幕府が衰退し、日本全国で大名という有力者が覇権を競い戦い合っていました。大名は自らの領国を豊かにするために、進んで京都の文化を取り入れます。その過程の中で「雅」が全国に広がっていったのです。

　17世紀に、江戸（現在の東京）が日本の行政の中心になった後も、朝廷は京都にありました。江戸や大阪は当時の経済の中心として、躍動的な町人文化が栄え、それに押されるように京都の文化は衰退してゆきました。

　しかし、「雅」という美意識はその後も受け継がれ、今では古都京都の美しさそのものを指すようにもなったのです。そして、戦国時代以来、各地に広がった染物や陶磁器などの工芸に代表される京都の文化は、今なおそれぞれの地域で保存され、多くの人が地方に根付いた「雅」な伝統を守っているのです。

色

　儒教道徳の影響を強く受けた武士を除けば、日本人は一般的に性に対して開放的でした。「色」とは、絵の具の「色」という意味の他に、恋や性を示す言葉として、今なお使われています。

*prudish［形］上品ぶった

imperial court was **in** direct **contrast to** the culture of *tsuya* of the common people represented in wood block prints (*ukiyoe*).

During the latter half of the 15th century and into the 16th century, Japan went through a period of almost constant war. During that time, the **central government** in Kyoto went into decline, as the *daimyo* ("**regional lords**") came to dominate the politics of the country. In their quest for power, the *daimyo* sought also to **bring into** their own domains the culture of Kyoto, and it was through this process that *miyabi* **spread throughout** Japan.

Even after the central government moved to Edo (present day Tokyo) in the early 17th century, the imperial court remained in Kyoto. During this period, Edo and Osaka became the economic centers of Japan and the **culture of the townspeople** flourished, while that of Kyoto faded.

The sense of beauty found in *miyabi* did not disappear, however, and even now when one hears the word *miyabi* one thinks of the elegance of the culture of old Kyoto. After the wars of the 15th and 16th centuries, **dyeing** and **pottery** and other **handicrafts** of Kyoto spread throughout the country, and today they continue to be strongly rooted in the local communities.

Erotic

Excluding the prudish* Confucian attitudes of the samurai, the Japanese have in general tended to be **open-minded** about sex. In Japanese, *iro* refers not only to color but can also refer to love or sex.

　色恋沙汰といえばセックススキャンダルのことですが、江戸時代も、庶民は色恋沙汰が大好きで、それが当時の歌舞伎や文楽といった芸能の**題材**になり、浮世絵でも取り上げられました。

　当時の幕府は、そうしたテーマを扱うことを**規制します**が、人々はその**網の目**をかいくぐって逞しく創作活動を続けたのです。

　「色」は「艶」にも通じ、都会人のお洒落なライススタイルとして支持された概念です。

　たとえば、春画と呼ばれる浮世絵があります。これは、江戸時代のポルノといってもよく、男女の交わりの様子が克明に描かれたもので、今では貴重な絵画として日本のみならず、世界で高価な**値段がつけられ**ています。

　江戸時代、庶民は**奔放に**「色」の世界を楽しんでいたのでしょう。

　そして今でも、日本を訪れた外国の人は、日本の開けっぴろげな**風俗産業の隆盛**ぶりにびっくりするそうです。

　実際、性に対するタブーの多いキリスト教やイスラム教の影響の少ない日本では、「色」という概念はそのまま人々に受け入れられ、性のテーマは漫画などでも頻繁に**取り上げられ**ています。

　「色」は、日本人の美意識の一部として認知されているのです。

The Japanese of the Edo era also liked their sex scandals, and these scandals were often used as the **subject matter** for the *kabuki* or *bunraku* (puppet) dramas.

The government at the time had regulations in place to **restrict** dramas using such themes, but **loopholes** were found and the production of these dramas continued to flourish.

Iro can also be seen as an element of being refined (*tsuya*), as part of the drinking and night-life culture of the big city.

For example, there are wood block prints (*ukiyoe*) known as *shunga*. These prints, essentially the pornography of the Edo era, today **fetch** high prices on world markets as precious examples of a unique form of Japanese art.

It seems that the common people enjoyed the world of *iro* **without restraint** during the Edo era.

When non-Japanese visit Japan, it seems that they are often surprised at the openness and **prosperity** of the country's **"pleasure" industry**.

Japan has little of the influence of Christianity or Islam and their taboos on subjects related to sex. Being more open-minded, it is common in Japan to **take up** themes related to sex in *manga* or other popular forms of entertainment.

For the Japanese, *iro* is seen as one aspect of their overall sense of beauty.

粋

　粋とは、「色」や「艶」の世界を心得えて、人生を生きる人を表す言葉です。これはある意味で、江戸時代にあった都会的なダンディズムといえましょう。また、気の利いた**気配り**や、**為政者**の庶民の気持ちを理解した判断なども「粋」という言葉で表現されます。

　たとえば、母親の病気の薬を買うお金ほしさに盗賊の盗みの手伝いをした者がいたとして、江戸時代に司法長官であった町奉行がその者の罪を赦して仕事を与えたとします。庶民はそれを「粋」なはからいといって**喝采する**のです。

　「粋」とは、小さなことでありながら、センスがよくアクセントの利いたことを示します。この事例の場合、町奉行が法制度を変革しようとすることは職務であって「粋」なことではありません。この各論でのかわいそうな犯人を救った小さな判断が「粋」なのです。

　同じように、たとえば部屋の中の小さな花瓶に**椿**をひと折り入れておいたとしましょう。それは大きな花の飾り付けではありませんが、訪れる人にちょっとした安らぎと**季節感を与え**ます。それが「粋」なアレンジなのです。

　「粋」なことは決して**雄弁**であってはなりません。それはささやかで、目にはつくものの、普段なら気づかないようなことにちょっとした工夫や心遣いが施されているものが「粋」なのです。

Chic

A person who is *iki* understands the worlds of *iro* and *tsuya*. It may be said that *iki* represents the "dandyism" of the Edo era. *Iki* can also be expressed in the **thoughtfulness** of one person towards another, for example in how **people in authority** might understand the needs of the common people in making judgments.

Let's say that in the Edo era, a person helped out with a robbery in order to buy medicine for his sick mother, and the judge, rather than sending the guilty person to prison, arranged a job for him. This would be **applauded** by the common people as an act of *iki*.

While an act of *iki* is usually small in scale, it has good sense and a strong impact. In the example used here, the judge is not trying to bring about a major change in the law; he is simply trying to help one unfortunate person, and that is why this is a case of *iki*.

In the same way, let's say that we displayed a single **camellia** in a small vase. Even though this is a small display of a single flower, it gives people coming into the room a sense of peace, while also **signaling the season**. This would be an example of an *iki* arrangement.

When being *iki* it is not necessary to be **eloquent**. One can be *iki* by doing a small thing to bring attention to something that would usually not be noticed.

妖

　「妖」とはこの世に存在しないような不気味な美しさを示す言葉です。たとえば、「妖艶」といえば、人を誘惑する女性の悪魔的な美しさを指します。

　日本の「美」を語るとき、そこに「死」のテーマが見え隠れすることが多々あります。もともと、武士道などで美しく死ぬことが美徳とされていたこともありますが、それに加えて仏教での来世観が、人の魂が不滅で、**この世に執着のある魂**は、その人の死後もこの世をさまようものとされたことが、文学や能などの伝統芸能などで死者の霊魂が頻繁に取り扱われた理由となります。

　第9章の「ものの哀れ」の項で、日本人は桜が美しく咲き、あっという間に散ってゆくことにその美しさをみると説明しました。そこには**潔く死ぬこと**の美学がメタファーとして隠されています。

　そうした「死」の陰に、人を惹きつける霊的な美しさが漂うものが、「妖」という言葉で表現される世界なのです。

　「妖」は「妖怪」の「妖」でもあります。妖怪とは西欧風にいえば悪魔のようなものですが、人の死後、その強い霊魂が怨霊となり、自然界のさまざまなものに化けてみたり、元々民間信仰の中で霊能があると信じられていた狐などの動物が奇妙な姿に化けて現れたりするものが「妖怪」です。

　「妖」とはこのような超自然的で**不気味な**ものを表現する言葉でもあるのです。

Bewitching

The word *yō* **connotes** a strange beauty that does not exist in this world. For example, the related word of *yōen* describes the demon-like beauty of a woman seducing a man.

When speaking of "beauty" in Japan, the theme of "death" is often just below the surface. One reason may be that in the samurai's world of *bushidō*, it was seen as a **virtue** to die a beautiful death. There is also the influence of Buddhism, where the sad beauty of death—reflected, for example, in the **wandering souls** of those unable to go to the next world—is a common theme in literature and drama.

In Chapter 9 we touched on *mono no aware,* the **sad beauty of the transient**, as seen in the brief time cherry blossoms are in bloom on the trees before being blown off. The cherry blossoms are a metaphor for the aesthetic of a **glorious death**.

The spiritual beauty hidden in the attraction to death is expressed in the word *yō.*

The Chinese character for *yō* is also used in the word *yōkai*. In the West, *yōkai* would be translated as a "demon-like creature." In Japan, *yōkai* is used to refer to the vengeful spirits of people who have been transformed after death into foxes and other animals.

In this way, *yō* is used to describe that which is very pure in nature and **eerie** or strange.

幽玄

　「わび」や「さび」の概念で、飾り気の無い素朴なものや、古く朽ちたものをじっと鑑賞していると、そこに時を超えた不思議な**奥深さ**を感じることがあります。その情緒を人々は「幽玄」と呼んでいるのです。

　また、日のかげりや夕暮れ時に漂う**不安定な闇**など、自然界の微妙な移ろいの向こうに感じる宇宙の**深淵**にもつながる静寂も「幽玄」の意味するところです。

　深遠なる静寂はまた「妖」なる世界でもあります。というのも、「わび」や「さび」は、永遠の時の流れの中で風化し、朽ちてゆくものへの愛着を語る言葉であり、それは「無常」の概念に従って、死にゆくことへの美学にもつながっているからです。

　中世以降日本人に親しまれてきた伝統芸能である「能」は、まさにこうした美しさを追求した舞踏劇で、その多くに死者の霊魂が語る場面がもうけられています。

　「幽玄」とは、日本人の抱く美意識の中でも、最も伝統的で**洗練された**美しさへの価値観であるといえましょう。

風流

　月見というイベントがあります。中秋の名月とは、澄んでひんやりとした秋の空気の中にみる満月の美しさを指す言葉で、そんな月を**愛でる**ことを月見というのです。

Profound Tranquility

As discussed in the sections on *wabi* and *sabi*, when one closely observes the old and decaying or that which is of extreme simplicity, one can be moved beyond time to feel a surprising **profundity**. This is called *yūgen*.

Yūgen may also be found in the **uneasiness** felt at the end of the day as darkness approaches, or in the subtle changes of the natural world as one looks into the tranquility and the **abyss** of space.

A profound tranquility is also part of the world of the bewitched (*yō*). In this same way, *wabi* and *sabi* are also connected to the aesthetic of death, as these sensibilities reflect the eternal passage of time and with it, decay and decline and the eventual transience to death.

The traditional Noh drama, a part of Japanese culture since the Middle Ages, places importance on this particular sense of beauty, often including scenes where the spirits of the dead speak of their trials.

It may be said that *yūgen* is a very traditional and **refined** aspect of the Japanese sense of beauty.

Cultured

In the autumn there is an event called *tsukimi*. *Chūshū no meigetsu* refers to the beauty of a full moon viewed on a clear autumn night; it also refers to the event itself of **admiring** the

こうした伝統的な**美意識を体験する**ことを、日本人は「風流」と表現します。

　この章に記した日本人の美意識をもって物事を鑑賞し、それを楽しむことが「風流」なことで、そうした行為を日本人は洗練されたものと感じるのです。

　「風流」を体得し、それを**実践できる**人は「風流人」と呼ばれ、文化人として尊敬を集めます。

　「風流」とは風の流れと書きますが、その表記の通り、風が流れるように**さりげなく**、心地よく日本の伝統美を表現できる人こそが「風流人」であるといえるのです。

　そうした意味では「風流」は「粋」にも通じる概念で、それは日本人が**あこがれる**感性であり、ライフスタイルです。

　もちろん、風流な人は美意識が洗練されているだけでなく、「徳」がある教養人となります。すなわち、日本人がよしとする価値観を体得し、それを美的なセンスをもって優雅に表現できる人が「風流」な人なのです。

moon in such fashion. The Japanese call the **experience of appreciating** such a sense of beauty *fūryū*.

Observing things with the Japanese sense of beauty, as described in this chapter, and enjoying that experience is *fūryū*. The Japanese consider such behavior to be very refined.

One who understands the true meaning of *fūryū* and who is able to **put it into practice** is called a *fūryūjin* and is respected as a person of culture.

The Chinese characters for *fūryū* mean "flow with the wind," and indeed a true *fūryūjin* is one who, like the movement of the wind, is able to express his appreciation of traditional Japanese beauty **in a seemingly effortless way**.

In this sense, *fūryū* is closely related to the concept of *iki* ("chic"). Both of these qualities are much **admired** by the Japanese.

It is true of course that a *fūryūjin* is not only a person with a refined sense of beauty; he must also be an educated person of principle. In other words, a *fūryūjin* is a person who has a strong grasp of the basic values and aesthetic sensibilities of the Japanese and who is able to express those values in an elegant and refined way.

14

流

Drifting Away

融通

　例えば、人がお金を借りたとき、「あの人に融通しても
らった」といいます。それは、貸した人がお金を必要な借
主のために、心を開いて**柔軟**に対応したことを暗に示して
います。ということで、この言葉は昔から金銭に関わる言
葉として使用されることが多かったのですが、そこにはも
う一つの隠れた意味がありました。

　あの人は融通のきく人だと言えば、**物分かりいい人**だと
いうことを示していたのです。つまり、融通とは柔軟性を
も意味した言葉だったのです。その反対に法律や決まり
事に従って、柔軟性なく決まった通りにしか物事を進めら
れないことを**杓子定規**な人といって、人々はその対応を嫌
いました。

　その昔、日本では杓子定規ではなく、相手の状況や心
情、さらに背景や置かれている立場などを理解して、例え
法律上は問題があっても情で物事を判断し、社会をうまく
進めてゆこうという考え方がありました。それが、融通と
いう価値観だったのです。融通は硬い制度と、**人情**の間に
立って、社会をうまく進める潤滑油の役割を示した価値観
だったのです。

　しかし、最近になって、こうした発想が社会での**公平な
判断**に支障をきたすということから批判されるようになっ
たのです。そして、賄賂や特定の人への利益を優先さ
せることを戒め、より公正な社会を目指す中で、融通とい
う考え方はむしろ避けられるようになってしまいました。

Accommodating

As an example, when someone loans us money, we may say, "She accommodated me." This is a tacit indication that the person who loaned money to the borrower was kind and **flexible**. In the past, this expression was most frequently used in connection with financial help, but there was another, less apparent meaning involved.

To say that a person was accommodating or flexible implied that the person was **understanding**. That is, accommodating also conveyed the meaning of flexibility. The opposite was someone who was strict and inflexible, who followed laws and regulations and who was **rule-obsessed**, the type of person that most people found to be incompatible.

In ancient times, Japan was not obsessed with rules. It was felt that society would progress best by taking into account the other person's situation and feelings, the background and the position in which the other person was placed. Even in the case of something that had to do with laws, decisions would be made by taking feelings into account. This was the value of "accommodation." This flexibility stood between strict systems and **human emotions** and was the sense of values that functioned to reduce friction, to smooth things out, so that society could operate smoothly.

However, in recent times this way of thinking has come under criticism in society as bring about obstacles to **unbiased decision-making**. With an eye to creating a just and impartial society which prohibits bribery and grants priority that benefits certain people, the idea of accommodation has fallen out of

しかし、そのことで、社会の中の潤いがなくなり、潤滑油によってちょっと調整をしようという判断ができにくくなっているのも事実です。融通という考え方のプラスの部分が失われるなか、世の中はだんだん**世知辛く**、人の心への配慮が少なくなってきていると思っている人が多いのも事実です。

忖度
<small>そんたく</small>

忖度とは、人の心を**推し量って**判断したり、時には扶助したりする考え方を指す言葉です。もともと融通と共に、忖度はそれほどマイナスの意味を持った言葉ではありませんでした。

しかし、近年、政治の世界で仲間うちの**利権**や権力の維持のためにこの発想が使われてきたことが社会問題になって以来、忖度はどちらかというと否定的な価値観と捉えられようになりました。

どんな価値にもプラスの部分とマイナスの部分があることは誰でも知っていることでしょう。しかし、そのマイナスの部分が強調され過ぎた時、その価値観自体が糾弾され、壊されてしまうこともあるのです。

例えば、「あの人にはお世話になったから、あの人の子どもに苦労をさせたくない」と言って、大学の入学試験の時に特別にその子どもの入学を許可すれば、それは**公私混同**で違法行為にすらなってしまいます。その時、忖度してしまったと言って糾弾された人は、社会に対して謝罪する

favor. However, as a result, at the same time social leeway and warmth has decreased, and in fact the smooth relations that previously allowed slight adjustments are no longer present in the making of decisions. As the positive elements in the concept of accommodation have disappeared, many feel that the world has gradually **become a harder place to live** and consideration of the feelings of others has decreased.

Intuiting the Unspoken

The term *sontaku* indicates the making of a decision by **surmising** someone's feelings and sometimes providing assistance that is unrequested. Initially, along with *yūzū*, the word did not carry a significantly negative nuance.

However, in recent years, this way of thinking has become socially problematic because it has been sued as a means of preserving **vested interests** and power among political circles. As a result, *sontaku* has come to be seen as a rather negative social value.

Most people surely grasp the fact that every social value has both positive and negative aspects. However, when the negative aspect is overly emphasized, that value itself is denounced and the whole value is done away with.

For example, consider a case where someone who is in a position of authority at a university has been kindly treated by another person and thinks, 'He has done so much for me in the past that I would not want his child to suffer in any way.' When the child is taking an entrance exam to that particular

わけです。しかし、お世話になった人の子どもに良いこと
をしてあげようという行為は、伝統的には、**恩に対して報
いる**という日本の前向きな価値観だったのです。しかし、
それを社会の制度を曲げて運用するときに、忖度の負の部
分が出てくるわけです。

　今、日本では、伝統的な価値観の負の部分が削除される
中で、人々の心持ち自体に変化がおきています。日本人が
古来持っていたアイデンティティが失われることへの危
機感を持っている人も多くいるはずです。忖度という価
値観のプラスの部分を育ててゆくにはどうしたらいいの
かは難しい課題です。教育や社会を通して人と人との関
わり方そのものへの探究が必要です。是は是、非は非とし
ながら、昔からの潤いある社会をどう維持してゆくか。今
ちょうど日本人にはそうした課題が突き付けられている
のかもしれません。

癒し

　世の中が、融通がききにくく、お互いへの配慮や思いや
りに基づいた忖度がしにくくなれば、当然人々は**心の余裕**
を失ってゆきます。近年、世界経済の中で日本が低迷し、

university, the first person wants to arrange to have the child specially admitted. This would be an instance of **mixing public and private matters** that could even become a matter of illegal activity. In this case, the person denounced for *sontaku* then has to apologize to society for his actions. However, from the traditional perspective, the person who was attempting to do something that would benefit the child of the person he was indebted to was motivated by the Japanese positive value of **repaying an obligation**. However, when that personal sense of value is put to practice in tweaking the social system, the negative aspect of *sontaku* comes to the forefront.

In present day Japan, as the negative parts of traditional values are being eliminated, people's frame of mind is changing. Many Japanese may sense an impending crisis at losing their long-held identity as Japanese. How one is to deal with the positive aspects of *sontaku*, which have been cultivated in society, has become problematic. It is necessary to examine the way in which people interact with one another through education and society. While approving right and condemning wrong, should one maintain the means of reducing friction that have been passed down through the ages? Japanese may well be confronting this type of issue today.

Peace of Mind

As the world around us becomes less accommodating (*yūzū*) and there is less intuiting of unspoken desires (*sontaku*), people naturally lose a degree of **peace of mind**. In recent years, amidst

　所得が増えず、心にも余裕がなくなっている中で、人々の心の中に癒しという価値観を大切にすることが多くなりました。

　癒しとは、自然の中で疲れた心身を治癒したり、人間関係が緊張する中で、優しい言葉を掛け合ったり、時にはふと一人になって好きなことに**没頭**することで、心の痛みを回復することを意味しています。そして今、人によっては、日本の伝統的な価値観などへも目を向けて、失われつつある古き良きものへの**郷愁**にひたることに癒しを求めようともしています。

　秋に京都に紅葉を見に行ったり、江戸時代をテーマにした人と人との心のやり取りを描いた映画を観たり、伝統工芸に没頭したりという行為が90年代から現在まで、日本人の中に多く見られるようになりました。社会に余裕がなくなった分だけ癒しへの執着が深くなってきたのです。そして、さらにその延長には、今までただがむしゃらに組織のために働いてきたことへの反省も見られるようになったのです。仕事より自分や家族の癒しを大切にした価値観が認められるようになったのです。

　個人を大切にしようという考え方は、そのまま終身雇用などの伝統的な日本社会のあり方に**疑問を投げかけ**、制度そのものの見直しにも繋がるようになりました。癒しを求め、過去に当然だとされた価値観が見直されているにもかかわらず、その行為の向こうにちらほらと見えるのが、実は失われつつある日本人の伝統的な事柄への**憧れ**であるのは、考えてみれば不思議なことだといえそうです。

Japan's economic slump, in which there is no increase in wages and there is little peace of mind or emotional leeway, many people have been placing a high value on *iyashi*, emotional healing.

Iyashi refers to any number of things. It includes psychological and physical healing in natural settings, someone speaking kindly in the midst of stressful human interactions, occasionally becoming completely **immersed** in a favorite activity—anything that promotes healing and recovery from emotional stress. Some people now seek this kind of healing by immersing themselves in the **nostalgia** for traditional Japanese values.

One can see this in the number of people who travel to Kyoto to see the changing colors of autumn leaves, who watch movies depicting the Edo period and the human relations of that time in history, and who, since the beginning of the 1990s, have become devoted to traditional crafts. To fill the gap left by the diminished leeway within society, people have become obsessed with attaining *iyashi*. And as a sort of extension of this, one observes a variety of soul-searching vis-à-vis what has been a habit of working energetically for some organization. There is more recognition of placing less emphasis on work than on increasing one's own peace of mind and that of one's family members.

The idea of placing emphasis on the individual has **cast doubts** on what has been taken to be standard Japanese society, including the notion of lifetime employment, and has led to a reexamination of the system as a whole. In searching for *iyashi*, not only have the values of years gone by been reexamined, but one can find here and there a degree of **reverence** for the Japanese traditions that have been lost. When one thinks about this, it is quite a remarkable phenomenon.

ゆとり

　ゆとりとは、余裕のあることを意味する言葉です。そして現代人はこの言葉を金銭的な余裕よりも心の余裕を意味する言葉として使うようになりました。

　日本人は戦後の荒廃から立ち直るために、昼夜をおいて働き、社会を発展させました。その世代が**高度成長期**の日本を作り、その子どもたちはその恩恵によってバブル期の繁栄を謳歌しました。当時は会社や社会の繁栄を第一として、人々は仕事に没頭したのです。そしてバブルが弾け、さらにバブル世代の人々が親になり、その子どもである現在の若者が育ってゆきます。

　今を生きる若者の多くは、それまでの価値観に**懐疑的**です。むしろ成功しなくても、金銭的に豊かさを求めなくても、**それなりの幸福**の中で静かに生きることを求めます。それが今を生きる人々のゆとりという価値観です。教育の上でも、それまでの進学重視の**詰め込み教育**を否定した「ゆとり教育」という制度も一時ありました。この教育を受けた人々をゆとり教育世代といいます。彼らやその後に育った若者は、終身雇用という価値観も持たず、個人の生活を大切にします。そんな**達観**した感情を「悟り」と呼ぶ人もいるのです。それは、先に紹介した修行によって会得する悟りとは異なる新たな価値観といえましょう。

Leeway

Yutori has the meaning of leeway, ease, and a degree of latitude.
To present-day Japanese, *yutori* refers less to financial leeway
than to psychological ease.

In order to recover from the destruction of World War II,
the Japanese people had to work day and night to rebuild their
society. That generation created **the period of high economic
growth**. Their children celebrated the benefits and blessings
in the period that became known as the economic bubble. The
strongest images that remain of that period are companies and
employees totally absorbed in working hard. When the bubble
burst, the young generation had already become parents. In
turn, their own children are today's youth.

Many of today's young people are **skeptical** of the values
that have continue to the present. Rather than struggling to
succeed, they prefer not to seek financial affluence but rather
to pursue a life of **reasonable happiness**. Their values seek to
live a of ease in the present. In the realm of education, there
was a period in which *yutori kyōiku*—education with a degree
of leeway—rejected education that aimed at **cramming** in order
to pass harsh entrance exams to elite schools and universities.
Students who received their education during this period are
known today as the *yutori kyōiku* generation. Neither that
generation nor the one that followed hold to the values of lifelong employment. They place emphasis on personal life. Some
people refer to this **far-sighted view** as *satori*, enlightenment or
higher perception. This is the deep understanding attained by
discipline, which has been described elsewhere in this book, and

　そんな若者を**自尊心**や自己達成感がないと昔を生きた
人々は批判します。それがまさに日本流のジェネレーシ
ョンギャップなのです。しかし、バブル崩壊以降、日本経
済は低迷し、世界の中での相対的な地位も揺らいでいま
す。その影響で、貧富の差や教育の格差が社会問題とな
り、日本社会は決してゆとりのあるものではなくなりまし
た。であればこそ、若者の抱くゆとりや悟りといった価値
観の向こうに何が見えてくるのか。今後の日本社会にど
のような影響を与えるのか。それはまだ**未知の領域**なの
です。

忍
にん

　この言葉は、世界中で人気を博した忍者の「忍」に他な
りません。
　忍は「しのぶ」とも読みます。それは目立たず、辛いこ
とにも**耐えて**、自分の**役割を全う**することをよしとする価
値観です。もちろんこの価値観は本書で紹介した、謙遜や
修練、求道などという価値観に通じる日本人の心の持ち方
に深く関わります。
　しかし、面白いことに21世紀になってゆとりや悟りが
云々される中で、忍は「諦め」という言葉に置き換えられ
たように思えます。古い価値観の影響を強く受ける年配
者と、その人たちが作った社会とのギャップの中で若者が

one can call it an entirely new sense of values.

People in the past would be critical of these young people's lack of **pride and self-respect** and their lack of any sense of accomplishment. Beyond doubt this is a Japanese version of a generation gap. However, since the burst of the economic bubble, the Japanese economy has slumped and Japan's international economic ranking has been undermined. As a result, the gap between wealth and poverty and the gap in education have become social problems. Japanese society has certainly not become more relaxed. That being the case, what is the outlook beyond the *yutori* that young people embrace and the values of the *satori* generation? What kind of influence will they have on Japanese society from this point onward? This remains **unknown territory**.

Patience and Self-Restraint

The Japanese character *nin* is, obviously, the base of the word *ninja*, which has gained worldwide popularity.

Nin is also read as *shinobu*, which means to conceal the self, **endure** hardships, and **willingly fulfill one's role**. This value has of course been introduced elsewhere in this volume, and it is deeply embedded in the Japanese values of modesty (*kenson*), self-discipline (*shūren*), and seeking after truth (*gudō*).

Interesting enough, however, in the 21st century in connection with *yutori* and *satori*, *nin* has become a variety of replacement term for resignation (*akirame*). In the gap between themselves and the older generation which was strongly affected

悟るとき、過去の価値観に強い反発を持って行動するのではなく、変わらない社会への「諦め」、つまり現代流の諦観を持ってしまうのです。それが、物言わぬ現代を生きる人々の「忍」の姿かも知れません。

悟りも忍も、昔は**僧侶**や武士が修行の中で培い、日本人の価値観の根本を形成しました。しかし、そんな価値観が変化した現代の癒しの世界では、それはノスタルジックな**古き良き時代**の価値観だと思われています。黙って文句を言わず、忍ぶことが求道の精神だと思われていた昔と違い、今人々は強い自己主張はしないものの、サラリと転職し、集団のニーズより自分の思いを優先させてゆきます。忍ではなく、黙ってその場から自分の姿を消してゆくわけです。

とはいえ、現代を生きる人は言葉で主張はしないまでも、こうした行動によって立派に自己主張をしているのだと評価する意見がないわけではありません。

忍という価値観が、そうした新しい日本人の未来にどのように**馴染ん**でゆくのか、興味あるところです。

同調圧力

日本社会はもともと狩猟社会ではなく**農耕社会**でした。個人芸が重んじられる狩猟社会と比較すると、農耕社会で

by the older values and the society those values created, the younger generation has achieved a certain awakening or enlightenment which has led them to strongly rebel against the older values. Instead, they have **resigned** themselves to surviving in a society that does not change. In a sense, they have adopted a contemporary variety of philosophical endurance or resignation. It may be seen as an unspoken form of self-restraint (*nin*).

In the past, **Buddhist priests** and samurai cultivated *satori* and *nin* through ascetic practices and these molded the fundamental values of the Japanese people. However, in the present, where society embraces *iyashi*, those values are seen as nostalgic remnants of the **good old days**. As opposed to the past, in which remaining silent without complaining and simply enduring, which was seen as the correct path in the search for truth, although the current generations do not strongly assert themselves, they place priority less on salary and career moves and place more on their own feelings. Instead of endurance, they silently disappear from the scene.

Having said that, even though Japanese in the present day do not express themselves verbally, one can say that they are successfully expressing themselves through their actions.

It will be quite interesting to see how this value of *nin* will **permeate** the Japanese people in new ways in the years to come.

Pressure to Conform

In its origin, Japanese society was not a hunting culture, but rather an **agricultural society**. In contrast with hunting

は個人の権利や実力以上に、村の中でどのように協力して秋の収穫を享受するかに人々は注力してきました。しかも日本は**島国**でしたから、大陸国家のような大量の移民や他部族の侵入による生存競争とも無縁の社会を長い間維持してきました。そんな遺伝子を引き継ぎながら、それでも現代社会では若い世代を中心に、自分の**実力**を相手に示し、自らのニーズをしっかりと主張することが良いことだという観念も浸透しつつあります。そこには海外からの影響もあるでしょう。

　しかし、欧米社会などと比較すれば、日本人は他者の目を気にします。多数の人がある行動をとることを当然とすると、その発想に逆らってあえて自己主張をすることは回避しがちです。そんな見えない社会の圧力を**同調圧力**と呼んでいます。コロナ感染症が流行したとき、法的に規制されていなくても、誰もが同じようにマスクをしました。アメリカなどでマスクをしない人々の強い意思が表明されたとき、多くの日本人は欧米流の**個人主義的**な考え方に戸惑いを抱いたはずです。

　この同調圧力は、海外からみると**社会規範**を重視する礼儀正しい日本人の姿として映ったかもしれません。しかし、日本社会をみるならば、こうした同調圧力の末に社会全体が**全体主義**に傾きながら、戦争へと向かっていった過去があることを忘れてはなりません。堂々と物をいうことをはばむ見えない圧力は、人への**配慮**というプラスの面と、ダイナミックで多様な社会を創造しにくいというマイ

societies in which individual skill was considered important, in agricultural societies, cooperation with the village and enjoying the benefits of a shared autumn harvest were more important than individual rights. Moreover, because Japan was an **island country**, it survived for a long period without the struggle for existence experienced by continental peoples who faced large numbers of immigrants and different tribes. Although it inherited this tradition, present-day society—centered around the young generation—widely shares a sense that it is acceptable to directly exhibit their own **abilities** to others and to express their own needs. It is likely that this is due to influence from overseas.

However, in contrast with Western societies, the Japanese still remain quite concerned about how others view them. When, as a matter of course, it becomes necessary for a large number of people to take action, the Japanese avoid expressing themselves in a way that could be taken as going against the group's fundamental idea. This invisible social pressure is the **pressure to conform**. During the Covid pandemic, even when there were no legal regulations requiring the wearing of masks, people wore them because everyone else did. Observing countries like America, where some people strongly resisted the wearing of masks, many Japanese must have been puzzled by the insistence upon such an **individualistic** way of thinking.

From outside the country, the pressure to conform may have seemed like the **social model** emphasized by polite Japanese. However, when one examines Japanese society, this pressure to conform can turn into **totalitarianism**, which one cannot forget led Japan into war in the past. The power to invisibly impede speaking out has, on the one hand, a positive impact in emphasizing **consideration** of others. On the other hand,

ナスの面があるわけです。日本人にとってこのマイナスの面をいかに克服するかは、21世紀の世界の中で激しい競争を生きぬくための大きな課題でもあるのです。

沈思黙考

　日本人が沈黙に強いことはすでに説明しました。沈思黙考は、じっと黙って思索に耽ることを示す言葉です。古来、そんな姿は賢人の典型的な行動様式だとされてきました。そして、日本人は言葉にすることなく、行動して結果を出し、さらにそのことは他者にアピールせずにいることに美学を覚えてきました。儒教の言葉に「巧言令色、鮮なし仁」という言葉があり（☞p.200）、美しい言葉で表現し過ぎることは、誠意のない証拠であると解釈されました。控えめで、静かで、それでいて深い教養のある人のことを、人々は「奥ゆかしい人」と言って称賛していたのです。それが日本人独特の不言実行という価値観の原点となりました。

　とはいえ、昔に比べ、日本人ははるかに自己表現をするようになりました。スポーツ選手などが、勝利した時にガッツポーズをして全身で喜びを表現したりする行動も、最近では当たり前になってきています。会議などで目を閉じて黙って考えている姿は、陳腐化した古いタイプの日本人を示すステレオタイプとなっているかもしれません。また、「奥ゆかしい」という言葉に至っては今ではほとんど使われなくなってしまいました。

however, there is a negative aspect that makes it difficult to create a diverse society. For the Japanese, how one can suppress this negative aspect will be a major challenge in attempting to survive the harsh competition of the 21st century.

Lost in Contemplation

As explained elsewhere in this volume, Japanese are especially comfortable with silence (*chinmoku*). *Chinshi mokkō* refers to being silent and **absorbed in thought**. In ancient times, this was the mark of a truly wise person, a sage. Among Japanese, it was considered a **high principle** to show results through actions rather than words, and to do so with no intention of appealing to others. There is a Confucian saying to the effect that "He who gives you fair words feeds you with an empty spoon," meaning that elegant phrases alone are not honest proof of sincerity. If a person is **reserved**, soft-spoken, and has a deep understanding of learning, people would refer to the person as a "**modest** person." This fundamental principle was at the base of the essential Japanese distrust of mere words and deep trust in actual deeds.

Having said that, in comparison with the past, Japanese have become much more self-expressive. It has recently become much more common for athletes when they win a competition to **punch the air** in triumph, expressing their joy with their whole body. The old stereotype of Japanese sitting silently in a meeting with their eyes closed may be **obsolete**. And the reference to someone being gracefully self-effacing may no longer be common.

しかし、それでも日本人は、しっかりと声をあげて自己主張をすることはやはり稀なのです。あの同調圧力というベクトルが働けばなおさらです。沈思黙考や不言実行の美学は古いものとされながら、逆に自分の考えや思いを理路整然と雄弁に語ることは、やはり言い訳がましい軽率な行動と取られかねないのです。

伝統的な価値観が**形骸化**し、ただその行動様式だけが受けつがれるとき、社会は停滞してしまいます。今、そんな形骸化が危惧されているのがここに紹介した沈思黙考や不言実行の美学なのかもしれません。

洒脱と気っ風

江戸っ子気質という言葉があります。江戸は東京の昔の名前です。

18世紀末に100万都市にまで成長した江戸は、町人文化が栄えた活気ある街でした。江戸で快活に活動していた人々のことを江戸っ子といいます。彼らの間では**さっぱりした心意気**が好まれました。ストレートで着飾らず、少々おせっかいなほど他人にも**情に厚い**人々がもてはやされたのです。そんな人のことを**洒脱な人**といい、彼らは気前もよく細かいことにあまりくよくよすることを嫌いました。多少見栄っ張りではあるものの、お金が入れば気前よく人に振る舞い、困っている人がいれば貸し借りを抜きにさまざまな扶助をします。そんな行為を「気っ風がいい」と人々はもてはやしました。

However, it is still uncommon for Japanese to speak up, to express their thoughts. Even more potent is the force toward conformity. While the aesthetics of silent contemplation and dependence on actions rather than words belong to the past, the fluent and logically consistent expression of one's thoughts and feelings can still be taken as an indiscreet way of making excuses.

When traditional values turn into **mere formalities** and only the behavioral pattern is passed down, society grows stagnant. The apprehension that they may be turning into simple formalities may indicate the value of these concepts of *chinshi mokkō* and *fugen jikkō*.

Sophisticatedly witty

There is a unique characteristic referred to as *Edokko* spirit, Edo being the old name for Tokyo.

By the end of the 18th century, Edo's population had grown to one million. The city was prosperous and filled with the culture of the townspeople. Among them, an **open-hearted spirit** was much admired. Straightforward, unrefined, slightly nosy about the affairs of other people, yet **soft-hearted**, the ethos of the townspeople was widely acclaimed. Such people were referred to as **chic and sophisticatedly witty**. They were generous and did not fret over small details. While they might have been somewhat ostentatious or pretentious, when they had money, they generously entertained others. When someone was in need, they willingly offered money and other forms of support. Such

　日本の伝統的な美学といえば、今までに紹介したわびやさび、さらに幽玄といった伝統芸能にも通じたものが主流だと思われています。しかし、江戸時代以降、こうした気軽でユーモアや人情を重んじる人生の美学がもてはやされました。これは、身分が最も高いとされた武士ではなく、巷の町人の間で育まれ、明治以降も受け継がれた気質でした。

　とはいえ、今東京に昔ながらの江戸っ子がいるかといえば、それは稀になりました。現代社会では、そんな洒脱で気っ風のいい生き様を美学とすること自体が困難になっているのです。特に都市部では人と人との**疎外**が進み、アパートに暮らしていると隣の人が誰かもわかりません。見知らぬ人へのおせっかいは却って迷惑がられます。江戸が東京になって150年以上が経過した今、洒脱で気っ風のいいライフスタイルは物語の中の価値観となってしまったのです。

　現代社会は西欧文明が東洋のライフスタイルに変化を与えながらつくられました。その現象は日本でも同様で、そうした変化の中で失われつつある価値観の代表が、人と人とが人情で繋がる江戸時代の町人のものの考え方なのかもしれません。

actions were made much of as examples of **open-heartedness**.

Speaking of traditional Japanese **aesthetics**, we have elsewhere introduced *wabi* (a taste for the simple and quiet), *sabi* (subdued refinement), and *yūgen* (the subtle and profound) that is thought to permeate traditional performance arts. However, since the Edo period, the aesthetics of light-hearted humor and warm-hearted lifestyle became broadly popular. This aesthetic was not that of the high-status samurai class, but emerged in the quarters where the townspeople lived, and it was passed on following the Meiji period.

Although there is something of the *Edokko* remaining in Tokyo, it is rare. In present-day society, it is hard to support such an urbane, witty lifestyle as an aesthetic today. Especially in urban areas, people have become more and more **alienated** from one another and people living in apartments don't even know who their neighbors are. Sticking one's nose in other people's business is simply annoying and no longer acceptable. Edo became Tokyo more than 150 years ago, and the sophisticated, urbane character of the *Edokko* lifestyle is a sense of value found only in theaters today.

Contemporary society was formed from the impact of Western civilization on Eastern lifestyles. The phenomenon was the same in Japan. Representative of what was lost in this process might well be that open-minded, warm-hearted relationship between townspeople during the Edo period.

やばい

　つい最近まで、「やばい」という言葉は何か危険な状態にあったり、まずいことをしてしまったりしたときに使う表現でした。つまり、「やばいよ」といえば、深刻で困ったぞという意味のスラングだったのです。

　しかし、最近特に若者は感動したり、自分の感情や情熱がプラス方向に盛り上がったりしたときにやばいと言います。年配者は最初こうした言葉の変化に戸惑い、違和感を感じました。しかし、**言葉は時と共に変化する**のです。

　やばいという言葉を今を生きる人が使うとき、その背景には日本語自体への意識の変化がうかがえます。実は、昔は感動し、**高揚感**を覚えたときにはさまざまな表現がありました。しかし、現在、誰もがこうした多様な表現を一つにまとめて「やばい」という言葉で語ってしまいます。時には単に楽しい思いをした時にも「やばい」という言葉を使います。こうした言語感の変化は、バブルが弾けた頃から顕著になりました。例えば、「とても」とか、「非常に」という極端な状況を表現するときに、若者がそれらをすべてまとめて「超」という言葉を使い始めたのも90年代以降のことでした。試験を受けて「超難しかった」といえば、「手に負えないほど困難なことだった」ということになります。

　確かに言葉は時代によって変わってゆきます。現在江戸時代の武士の言葉を使う人は誰もいません。しかし、日本語の中の**繊細な**意味合いや感触を「やばい」という一言で片付けてしまう世代が増えていることに、言葉の現象だ

Super

Until quite recently, the adjective *yabai* was used to refer to dangerous, risky situations and it was applied to things that were awkward and disadvantageous. In other words, when someone described something as *yabai*, it was a slang way of describing serious trouble.

Nowadays, however, particularly young people use the term when they are impressed, in a positive sense to express their feelings or excitement. Older people were at first bewildered by that meaning and somewhat uncomfortable about how it was used. However, **words change with the times**.

When people today use words like *yabai*, they become aware that the background of the Japanese language is changing. In the past, when people felt excitement or an **upsurge of emotion**, there were various ways of expressing it. Now, however, people use a single word like *yabai* to express all of these feelings. On some occasions *yabai* is used to express joy or delight. This change in the view of language was particularly striking when the economic bubble burst. For example, *totemo* (very) and *hijōni* (really) came into use to express an extreme condition. Young people in the 1990s began combining both of those meanings into one word: *chō*, meaning "super" or "ultra." In explaining an exam as *chō-muzukashii* (ultra-hard) they meant that it was completely beyond their ability to pass.

To be sure, vocabulary changes with the times. No one uses the language of the Edo period samurai any more. However, in the fact that the **subtle** nuances and connotations of Japanese are reduced to a single word by people in one generation after

けではない、日本人の価値観の変化を感じている人も多い
のではないでしょうか。

映える

　スマートフォンで風景を撮影し、それをインスタグラム
にアップすることは、誰もがやっていることでしょう。ア
ップしたくなるような素敵な風景のことを、人々は「**イン
スタ映え**」すると表現します。早春の朝の膨らみかけた桜
の蕾や、夏陽に輝く花畑など、インスタグラムで人が「い
いね」をしそうの風景を「インスタ映え」というのです。

　　「 春は 曙（夜明けどき）、

　　　夏は夜、

　　　秋は夕暮れ、

　　　冬は早朝」

　これは11世紀の清少納言による随筆「枕草紙」の冒頭の
文章の一部です。そこではそれぞれの四季の中でどの時
間帯が好きかを作者は語ります。今流にいえば、彼女にと
ってのインスタ映えを感じるときのことを綴ったものと
いえます。もともと「映える」とは、時の流れの中で、目
に止まる**鮮やかな美しさ**を意味しています。それは瞬時
のことが多く、その直後には風景は移ろいます。

　元来、日本人は自然の変化の中に、世の中の**無常**を重ね

another suggests that one can find change not only in language but also in the values of Japanese as well.

Looking Attractive

Almost everyone today takes photos with their smartphones and uploads them to platforms like Instagram. People search for beautiful scenes and take photos of them, referring to them as "**Instagrammable**." In early spring mornings, they take photos of cherry blossoms beginning to bloom and in summer sunshine they do the same with fields of brilliant flowers. Any scene that might attract "likes" from viewers is "Instagrammable."

Spring at daybreak
Summer at night
Autumn at dusk
Winter at the break of day

This is from the opening passage of the eleventh century random musings titled "The Pillow Book" written by Sei Shonagon. The author includes her favorite time of day in each of the seasons. In modern terms, it can be said that she sets down the parts of the days that are Instagrammable. Originally the term *haeru*, appearing attractive, carried the meaning of something of **graceful beauty** that catches the eye within the flow of time. In many cases, it lasts just an instant, and immediately afterward the scene fades.

Originally, the Japanese attempted to capture within the

てみるセンチメンタリズムを和歌や俳句、さらに詩や随筆の中に記してきました。現代人がそれをインスタグラムによって追いかけるのは、癒しの追求の延長かもしれません。枕草紙が執筆された平安時代から現在まで、「映える」ものへの感傷、そして「映える」ものが移ろうことからくる無常観などが日本人の心の奥底に受け継がれてきました。典型が「夕映え」という言葉です。それは夕陽が沈む直前に自然が放つ鮮やかな風景を指しています。

　世界中のどこの国にも独自で美しく特殊な文化があり、日本もそんな世界の仲間の一つです。日本は山の多い島国で、四季があり、文明が育まれた日本の数少ない平地や盆地は照葉樹林帯に属していました。そんな背景の中で、大陸とも交流しながら日本人は独自の文化を育み、世代から世代へとつないできました。「映える」ことへの日本人の執着は、そんな日本人を取り巻く自然環境と、そこに持ち込まれた**仏教観**などが関わって培われました。

　こうした日本人の**感性**は伝統的な芸術やアニメなどの現代アートに反映され、世界の人々から注目されました。「映える」ことは、平安時代からコンピューター世代に至る日本人の心を象徴する価値観だといえそうです。

changes of seasons in nature the **impermanence** of the world and portray it in waka, haiku, poems, and miscellaneous writings. In today's Instagram images, people may be pursuing a similar kind of peace of mind (*iyashi*). The **sentiments** that are recorded in "The Pillow Book" during the Heian period and are still sought today may indicate that in the depths of the minds of the Japanese there is an inherited consciousness of the mutability of the world. A classic example of this is the word *yūbae*, evening glow. It refers to the dazzling natural color that the sun gives off just before it sets on the horizon.

Every country has its own unique, distinctive culture, Japan among them. Japan is an island country with many mountains, four distinct seasons, and a culture that was created in its numerous flatlands and valleys surrounded by evergreen broadleafed forests. Against this background, while Japan carried on exchanges with the continent, the Japanese created their own culture and one generation passed it on to the next. Japanese people's attachment to *haeru* was nourished by the natural environment that surrounded them as well as the **Buddhist views** that were brought in from the continent.

Such Japanese **sensibility** is reflected in the traditional arts, anime, and other forms, and these attract the attention of people around the world. The notion of *haeru*, showing things to advantage, is a sense of value that symbolizes the spirit of the Japanese—from the Heian period to the computer era.

English **C**onversational **A**bility **T**est

国際英語会話能力検定

● E-CATとは…

英語が話せるようになるための
テストです。インターネット
ベースで、30分であなたの発
話力をチェックします。

www.ecatexam.com

● iTEP®とは…

世界各国の企業、政府機関、アメリカの大学
300校以上が、英語能力判定テストとして採用。
オンラインによる90分のテストで文法、リー
ディング、リスニング、ライティング、スピーキ
ングの5技能をスコア化。iTEP®は、留学、就職、
海外赴任などに必要な、世界に通用する英語力
を総合的に評価する画期的なテストです。

www.itepexamjapan.com

［日英対訳］**日本人のこころ** 増補・改訂版
Heart & Soul of the Japanese

2023年 8 月 4 日　第 1 刷発行

著　者　　山久瀬 洋二

訳　者　　マイケル・クーニー

発行者　　浦　晋亮

発行所　　**IBCパブリッシング株式会社**
　　　　　〒162-0804 東京都新宿区中里町 29 番 3 号 菱秀神楽坂ビル
　　　　　Tel. 03-3513-4511 Fax. 03-3513-4512
　　　　　www.ibcpub.co.jp

印刷所　　**株式会社シナノパブリッシングプレス**

ISBN978-4-7946-0769-0